From Seekers
to Finders

Other New Freedom Press titles
by Satyam Nadeen

FROM ONION TO PEARLS: *A Journal of Awakening and Deliverance*

BEYOND ENLIGHTENMENT: *Abiding in the Zone*

These books are available at your local bookstores
or may be ordered directly from:

New Freedom Press
P.O. Box 1496
Conyers, GA. 30012
Telephone: 888-363-3738
Fax: 770-785-9260

Please visit Nadeen's website at:
www.satyamnadeen.com

From Seekers to Finders

~❧~

The Myth
and Reality
about
Enlightenment

SATYAM NADEEN

Published and distributed in the United States by:
New Freedom Press, P.O. Box 1496 Conyers, GA. 30012
Telephone: 888-363-3738 Fax: 770-785-9260

Design: Jenny Richards

THE HEART OF AWARENESS by Thomas Byrom, © 1990. Reprinted by arrangement with Shambhala Publications, Inc., Boston.

Library of Congress Cataloging-in-Publication Data

Nadeen, Satyam.
    From seekers to finders : the myth and reality about enlightenment / Satyam Nadeen.
        p. cm.
    ISBN 1-56170-588-8 (pbk)
    1. Spiritual life. I. Title.

BL624 .N28 2000
291.4'4--dc21   99-047549
                                         CIP

                    ISBN 1-56170-588-8

            03 02 01 00   4 3 2 1
        First Hay House Printing, January 2000
              This Printing, May 2004

        Printed in the United States of America

Contents

Introduction

Whenever an author's first book is successful, there is usually a publisher's request for a sequel. However, most sequels seem like the "same old same old," just somewhat rehashed in a new format. However, if I have to discipline myself and spend all the time it takes to get a whole book together, then I'd better say something new and exciting and add to the original message. I believe that I am now at that precise point in this evolving "seeker to finder" message.

When *From Onions to Pearls* came gushing through my pen, I was still in a federal penitentiary at the very beginning of my own wake-up call, still in the bliss-ninny stage of my rapture. The only words available to me were those that described my own personal waking-up experience. Maybe that was interesting to some seekers, but what if this was only an isolated event, brought on by harsh, violent, inhuman prison conditions that crush the ego but are totally unavailable to the ordinary seeker? What about the normal seekers who don't live in these extremes? How do they wake up? This book addresses those individuals.

But first, let me bring you up to speed by sharing my personal story. *Onions* was first published in August of 1996, the very month I was released from the penitentiary. Before I had completed my required six months of halfway house confinement, the second 5,000 copies were printed, and since then there have been two subsequent printings. But that first printing found its way into the hands of seekers already moving imperceptibly into this fourth-dimensional Shift before they had even read the book (I define the *Shift* in chapter 1). This in turn created a network of energy vortexes in cities throughout the world where I was invited to facilitate three-day weekend intensives, once I was allowed to travel. In fact, the very weekend I was released from the halfway house, we started in Santa Fe and have averaged three out of four weekends per month ever since all over the globe.

Now, here is the sequel worthy of writing! This is a feedback sequel, generated from the thousands of other seekers who have been sharing their own experience in countless Satsang circles (where two or more seekers gather to share their sacred truth). An incredible source of new information is now available to relay to you. The first book was about my wake-up—no big deal! This book, however, will grab your interest big-time because it is the first book I am aware of that openly shares what is really happening right now in the so-called Millennium Shift, which was foretold by not only Buddha, but also the Mayan and Hopi Indians. Part of this sharing involves dealing with the outrageous and very funny concepts that virtually all seekers have about what it means to be "awake" or "enlightened" these days as they get swept away by the force of this Shift.

We had fun together in *Onions,* and maybe it got you wondering about old, worn-out concepts such as karma, reincarnation, free will, creating your own reality, and so on. It may even have opened you up to the possibility of a pathless, goal-less, do-nothing-to-self-realize attitude and understanding about your life and why you are even here to begin with. It's time to move on, with your trusty field guide and investigative reporter here bringing you the warming and wonderful facts about everyone else's transition from having both feet in the third dimension to having one foot move into the fourth. And that is an interesting report to write!

~≈≫~

chapter 1

The Awakening

Just in case you haven't yet read in *From Onions to Pearls* how this story all began, I will quickly recap. Even those who have read it before are now in a different space of awareness, and just as the river's water is never in the same place twice, neither are we when we hear wisdom, even some old familiar truism. People who participate in the intensive workshops that I give tell me that every time they reread *Onions,* it's almost like reading it for the first time. There are as many layers of the truth as there are old concepts and conditioning that you can peel away.

I guess I was a seeker from the git-go. At the ripe old age of 12, I entered the seminary to become a Catholic priest and pursued this course till I was 26. Somehow the priesthood, Catholicism, and Western mysticism just didn't deliver what I was longing for at this point. So I left and went down the Eastern spiritual road with all the traditional disciplines such as yoga, meditation, guru-hopping, and hanging out in ashrams.

Along with these, I was very much into all the self-help, life-enhancement courses and workshops that spiritual psychology had to offer. But instead of getting closer to the Promised Land, I was fading farther away in all my attempts to catch the brass ring of self-realization.

The closest I came to knowing who I was lay in a little white pill called MDMA, or Ecstasy. My greatest regret was that its door would slam shut after only a few hours, leaving me yearning even more for the oneness, peace, and total absence of fear that those few hours had encapsulated. I made it my life's mission to get this little marvel of instant, short-term enlightenment out to as many millions of people around the globe as possible. When it became illegal in the U.S.A. in 1985, the operation moved to South America with distribution in the European countries where it was still legal. But as destiny would have it, in spite of the best-laid plans of mice and men, some of it slipped through the cracks back into the U.S.A., and under our conspiracy laws, that meant that I was held responsible by the Drug Enforcement Administration (DEA). The judge gave me 87 months in a federal penitentiary, and there you have it. You can read the details in *Onions* if so inclined.

But before I go any further into my personal awakening, let me give a few definitions—a new vocabulary is needed to describe the Shift in concept-free semantics. I define the *third dimension* as "all of created reality that is perceived through the interpretation of the mind." The *fourth* is that which is beyond the third (and perhaps there are many more dimensions); it is perceived by the intuitive or heart function and understood by the presence of the inner Witness, which is beyond emotional reaction and simply observes with utter neutrality. The fourth dimension is the world of Spirit!

Being incarcerated was both my worst nightmare and my *dark night of the soul,* which is an idea originated by John of the Cross to describe a painful period of his spiritual growth. Within two years, a total and sudden Shift from the third dimension into the fourth occurred. Everything I had ever searched for, longed for, and had performed near-impossible feats to attain was simply and effortlessly opened up in my consciousness and personal awareness. I just woke up one day and remembered who I was, after a lifetime of searching.

But how does one "wake up"? I can only describe here the experience of my own awakening. I had already arrived at a point where I just flat-out gave up the search, realizing that I could never know with a limited and finite mind about this infinite Vastness that I had been searching for. At pretty much the same time, I also felt that even if I had known something, there still wasn't anything I could do about it.

Then I came across a phrase in Ramesh Balsekar's book, *Consciousness Speaks,* where he states that Consciousness is all there is, and *I am That!* Suddenly, on the spot, I remembered this truth at a level beyond any experience or knowledge. I actually knew it at a soul or essence level, maybe even a cellular level. It was as if I had been sleepwalking my whole life and thinking I was an entity separate from God and all others, when suddenly I just woke up and remembered that I am the Source of it all.

At that moment, my *deliverance* began, which is an automatic process that handles all the ramifications of this understanding. In your daily life, once you wake up and remember who you are, you can start the process of reversing all the old concepts and conditioning that have had you going sideways your whole life. In a flash of insight and remembrance—a very dark night of the soul—I went from a confused, lonely victim of this horrible third dimension to the total freedom, joy, peace, and clarity of the fourth. The *rapture* followed, which is the part of the Shift that feels like being swept away in the relief, safety, and freedom of being home at last.

So in this first flush of exploring the fourth dimension's everyday reality, I began writing in a journal that eventually turned into *Onions.* That book was an attempt to explain one man's new reality of living with one foot in the third dimension and the other in the fourth. The main ingredients were surprise and shock at how simple life can be in the fourth dimension. Add to that an overwhelming humor and amusement at how serious, mysterious, and complicated we've made this journey of spiritual seeking. It becomes hard to believe that we could ever hope to become a finder on our own.

This book leaves behind the awakening of Nadeen and focuses on the reality of the big Shift that is now taking place. Millions of seekers are ending up as finders in the fourth dimension, and they are hungry for up-to-date feedback from others who have made the Shift a few minutes ahead of them. The fact of the matter is that this has never happened before in the recorded history of time: We used to have a handful of awakened ones. Now we have millions! We don't really have any manuals readily available to us as a guide for living with a foot in each dimension. No one has ever accurately described what this awakening process actually consists of, apart from some glorified aspects of its freedom, which are only part of the equation.

In fact, up till now, if we were going to talk about the reality of this Shift, we only had old, tired concepts available about this new state of awareness. For a large part of this discussion, we will have to focus on the old myth of enlightenment if we are really ready to understand and accept what Is—just as it is.

chapter 2

~❧❦❧~

The Main Ingredients of Awakening

Because we are walking through a minefield of old concepts regarding just what a wake-up call involves, let's explore the basic elements of this Shift. The ancients in the Vedas and the *Bhagavad Gita* referred to the Source of All That Is as *Satchitananda,* which means "an eternal reality (Sat), in pure awareness (Chit), and in bliss (Ananda)." Like all energy, this Source pulses back and forth, in this case between the state of rest and the world of appearance. At rest, Source is completely aware and blissful as impersonal energy, but because it is the infinitely expanding Vastness, it cannot fully know itself as a personal energy. In order to know itself, it limited itself into a more finite object—by creating the manifested world of appearance, which I call the third dimension or the dream.

However, in this dream, we as individual mind/body organ-

isms are not the *dreamer* but the *dreamed.* We are the objects of
Source, the Subject. [EDITOR'S NOTE: Since all beings in this
manifested world are parts of the Source, we can each refer to
Source as "I" or "me," as is done below.] As energy that pulses,
Source has this dream on a breathlike pulsation, creating all manifestation on the inbreath, and on the outbreath, going back to rest
and effecting total dissolution. If you are ready to really stretch
your limited imagination, fancy this: The *Gita* says that God's
inbreaths and outbreaths each last for a duration of 311 trillion,
40 billion years in Earth-time and that this pulsation goes on for
all eternity. But who knows—time is relevant only in the third
dimension.

Once we can at least intellectually understand this description of Source, then we have cleared the path to someday getting
an intuitive hit of full memory and understanding, all the way
down to our essence and cellular memory level, knowing that
Consciousness is all there is, and *I am That.* The word *That* indi-
cates what is ineffable and indescribable about the Infinite
Vastness that is our own true nature.

As soon as this part of the Shift has happened in a way that
you actually begin to remember that you are the Satchitananda
that the ancients were describing, then a natural process that I call
the *deliverance* takes over. Its function is to explain at an inner
Satsang level what the ramifications are of this subtle, newly
found remembrance of your own true identity (*Satsang* means
"divine inner guidance"; see chapter 7).

It may even begin with the understanding of why you showed
up at all in this world of appearance. As Source at rest, it was
impossible to fully know yourself because you are infinite. How
do you connect the infinite to a knowable finite? By limitation!
That idea is missing from the pulsation of rest and infinite expansion. So I limited myself to a universe of minerals, plants, insects,
and humanoids. The fullest expansion that we can know in the
third-dimensional experience is the human emotions. Now please

notice that I did not say only the positive emotions—I mean *all* the emotions that arise from both love on the positive side and fear on the negative side. Am I talking about sides already? Of course I am, because in a world of appearance, what better way to limit oneself than for every single idea to have an opposite—and valid—counterpoint idea. That way, whatever you can say about one idea, its opposite is also true, and they can meet somewhere in the middle.

So: Source is having a nice long dream in which it writes a script that involves every living creature. These creatures are each unique, each with a different script to act out. This script covers every possible scenario within the framework of the human emotions. No possible extreme of emotion will be left out or not fully explored. And as the Source, who wrote the script's automatic laws of energy, I am now acting out each of all the possible roles. I am also present simultaneously in the middle of it all as the audience of Awareness, thoroughly enjoying myself, while getting to know myself better all the while.

There are, however, some practical ramifications of this dream world of appearance called the third dimension. Perhaps your own deliverance will point out to you the following realities:

1. There is neither an individual doer, nor free will on the part of this illusory doer in the third dimension. As for the fourth, well, that's another matter.

    You see, Source has infinite wisdom to draw on in this whole spontaneous dream to make it all seem so real. Could you really get into and hooked by all the negative emotions as a player in this dream if you didn't actually believe that it is all real? You have to feel that you are somehow a separated individual with free will and choice. You don't come here remembering how you got separated in the first place; you landed on the wrong planet without a clue as to how or why you got here, except that you feel this urgent longing to go "home."

But where is home? Your societal conditioning quickly fills in all the needed details with Source's purposeful disinformation, which keeps you in a state of constant confusion and contradiction about the meaning of life. All this conditioning assures Source that each individual will experience all emotions in a balanced way—equal freedom and limitation, equal positive and negative response in the dream world.

2.   The purpose of your life is to be a vehicle for Source to experience all the human emotions.

3.   Whatever is in this world of appearance is exactly the way it is supposed to be. Nothing needs to be fixed! Nothing is broken!

4.   There is no spiritual discipline that you can do to cause your own Shift. If and when it occurs, it happens in spite of you, never because of you. So just be! Do nothing! Understanding is all! Life is just as it is.

5.   Karma and reincarnation are concepts of the third dimension; they encourage the idea of a separated self who has free choice to do good or bad and be rewarded or punished in future lives.

6.   You are already "enlightened" by virtue of who you really are: You are Satchitananda, and just because you show up in a dream appearance doesn't change your essential nature.

7. There are no paths or goals in this world of appearance. Just show up, and you are already perfect just as you are—right in line with your own destiny.

8. Your personal story is part of a giant soap opera, which brings tears to the eyes of the audience and guarantees you an Oscar at the end.

9. For all control freaks out there, you are merely puppets in the dream of Source.

10. If Consciousness is all there is, and I am That,
    then everyone else out there must really be the same
    Consciousness as well. So where are my enemies now?

11. O death, where is your sting? I am an eternal reality!

12. As a manifestation of Source, I can't possibly screw up, miss out on my destiny, make a wrong choice, be a victim, or be held responsible for the sorry-looking state of affairs in my life and for the planet.

13. I am *most Divine* when fully engaged in my human predicament with all its seeming imperfections, foibles, negative emotions, and multiple daily contractions.

14. To be fully awake is simply to remember who
    I am. I am Satchitananda! I am the Source of all
    Consciousness, and that is all there is! *I Am That!*

chapter 3

The Shift in Mainstream Spirituality

When this Shift from third- to fourth-dimensional consciousness occurred for me, please keep in mind that I had been sitting for two years in an overcrowded prison cell trying to simply survive, not wake up. When it happened, though, of course I realized the significance—it moved me from total fear and panic into a state of immeasurable safety and relief. But there was still enough of my mind/ego/personality left to immediately grab on to this situation as "very special." Anything the mind sees as "special" is a red flag, as I was soon to find out in my deliverance. As it turns out, the very essence of this Shift involves living for the first time, after more than a half-century of striving to be "special," in a far more delicious, Jacuzzi-like feeling of just being *ordinary*. In fact, this is definitely one of the common denominators that our Satsang circles share: What a relief now to just be ordinary!

To move me through this old, stuck reaction of wanting to feel special again, the Shift spun out for me a crystal-clear vision regarding how it was affecting not only me but all other seekers as well. Mind you, I still didn't know what this Shift involved yet or where it was going, or even if it might ever end. But I saw clearly that it involved all seekers on the planet finding that they are each and all the Source of all Consciousness, the only absolute Reality there is. I saw and knew this as a new happening, not something far off in the future. That first vision was enough to change the need to feel special about all this into simple, total love and gratitude, to the point that it actually didn't matter anymore whether myself or anyone else ever Shifted. What changed was that I could experience the big picture now through the eyes and understanding of Source.

The next four years in prison provided me with all the time in the world to experience my own deliverance. The starting point of that first glimpse and understanding of the Shift brought me to a new level where I could then share in a Satsang circle, even among total strangers and with full confidence, what this all meant for me.

What I didn't know, though, was whether this Shift was a mainstream event affecting all other seekers. However, within a week of final release from prison, I was plunged into a nonstop Satsang tour almost every weekend. The format consisted of a Friday night introductory Satsang of at least two hours, which was open to the public. This was followed by an all-day Saturday and Sunday intensive for those who were interested in further exploring what it truly meant to live with a foot planted solidly in each dimension.

The very first tour was sponsored by Mary-Margaret Moore of "Bartholomew" fame in Santa Fe, New Mexico. Can you imagine how I must have felt that week, coming out of prison where all convicts are generally regarded by prison officials as the scum of the earth, into a hall full of beautiful, smiling, accepting people, eager to hear about the Shift? My voice was so weak and over-come by emotion that I could hardly speak. So far, I had told my tale of awakening to no one outside my own intimate circle in prison. There I was, in a huge hall full of people who were prob-ably expecting some enlightened sage to blow them away with profound insights or *shaktipat* (transmission of sacred energy), and I was still very much feeling the shame of six years of living in a prison hellhole. Not only that, I didn't have a clue about what to say or how to facilitate a three-day workshop about awakening. But that was a problem only for my mind, not for my heart. Enter the magical energy force field of Satsang, where mind doesn't dwell. From the depth of my experience of already having lived in the fourth dimension for four years, an effortless stream of com-munication flowed spontaneously and touched everyone there in the intuitive part of their understanding—not because of my words, but in spite of them. I looked out to see a whole room full of people nodding their heads in agreement, smiling in accord, and asking profound questions that sprang from the well of their own Shift. Then, during the intensive part of the weekend, those present told actual stories about their own unique and interesting process from being obsessive seekers to becoming relaxed find-ers. I recognized myself in each and every sharing that weekend.

In the early intensives, I limited the accounts of everyone's journey as seekers to more or less five minutes apiece so we could finish by lunch on Saturday. But after hearing thousands of such sharings, I realized that this was perhaps the most powerful process of all, and I started giving each one my chair to sit in and share their story without a time limit. What seems to happen is that while everyone's journey is absolutely one of a kind, a uni-versality does emerge that we can all relate to.

Would you like to hear some of the more common denomi-nators of the Shift? To close the chapter, consider the following, which have filtered through from all over the globe in the more than 70 intensives that I've led at the time of this writing:

1.   Seeking usually began with deep questions about God and life as a child.

2.   We felt somehow different and out of place early on as inhabitants of planet Earth. A stranger-in-a-strange-land kind of feeling, as if we landed on the wrong planet by mistake.

3.   We started with traditional connections to Christianity, and by our mid-teens, we had moved to more alternative investigations and spiritual practices.

4.   We felt we might find what we were longing for in a good relationship, so we got married and subsequently divorced—not just once, but in multiple attempts to find that perfect soulmate.

5.   Most of us had our first glimpse of this possible other reality when experimenting with mind-expanding drug trips. But like all relationships, this couldn't deliver full time.

6.   Then began an endless search through the New Age remedies that were coming into vogue then: Transcendental Meditation, yoga, Eastern gurus, trips to India, positive thinking, visualizations, affirmations, macrobiotic diets, and countless thousands of dollars spent on innumerable self-help workshops. Alas, none of these delivered the Promised Land.

7.   At some time in the last three to ten years, we slipped into what can only be called a dark night of the soul. Here, all our relationships and attachments—to family, careers, the love of our lives, hobbies, or art—started to

dissolve. This left us in a limbo of despair because while the third-dimensional pulls of conventional wisdom were fading away, we had not yet arrived at the full freedom of the fourth dimension.

8. Even worse than the emotionally deserted wasteland of this dark night was the intensity of longing that was building in us, seemingly without respite. To make it even more confusing, our bodies were being rewired to handle a higher frequency for the Shift. Common symptoms include: mild depression, chronic fatigue, weird aches and pains, electrical shocks running through the body, nervous breakdowns, short-term loss of memory, and strange tumors and cancers coming and going. Imagine—by all New Age standards, we had been taking excellent care of our bodies, yet they were breaking down, and we were running out of measures and energy to fix our lives one more time.

9. For those of us who had been devoted to a personal and perhaps living guru or spiritual teacher, there now occurred a realization that this person may indeed have been awakened, but that energy wasn't being transferred over to us by osmosis or their techniques of meditation. An addendum here from my own observations: It seems that anyone still attached to a guru (in the sense that they give their power away or hold that person aloft in any way as "special") is not yet ready to Shift. Somehow, the idea of anyone being so special keeps the illusion of separation alive and well.

10. After a lifetime of intentional effort, which seemed to work just enough to keep us hooked but not deliver, we now start to slowly drift toward a new understanding.

Maybe, just maybe, we are not the doers of our destiny after all.

11. Then we read a book or perhaps someone comes to town who explains that Consciousness is all there is, and *you are That!* You are not the third-dimensional doer—never were, never will be. Therefore, since you already are Satchitananda, maybe you don't have to do anything else to be who you already are and always have been.

12. Because this Shift is not generally a sudden or dramatic awakening, it takes trust that all is well, as it subtly directs our ancient memory to remember who we really are. Then our deliverance is directed to resonate more with the ramifications of this in our daily lives. Instead of thinking we are the doers, we now can just allow a non-doer attitude in the middle of any action. Thus, life just unfolds around us according to our manifest destiny, no longer needing intentional efforts to make it all happen.

chapter 4

Occam's Razor

William of Occam was a philosopher/scientist who lived about 600 years ago and made a profound scientific discovery while his contemporaries were still arguing about whether the sun circled the earth or vice versa. Some of you may remember his principle from the movie *Contact*.

Basically, it states that the simplest explanation for a phenomenon is virtually always correct. This principle has never yet been proven wrong, even in the face of all the new discoveries in quantum physics. So let's apply this now to the spiritual quest of moving from seekers to finders.

We start with the basic confusion of all seekers early on in their lives. We realize at some point that we have landed as a stranger on the wrong planet. We don't have a clue as to how we got here, why we are even here at all, or what exactly we are supposed to do about this deep longing to go "home" somewhere. We are then offered thousands of contradictory societal and religious theories about the do's and don'ts, shoulds and shouldn'ts of life, usually with an "or else"!

Western mysticism and Christianity can offer you a combination of heaven, hell, and purgatory; commandments and precepts; saints and sinners; original sin, mortal sin, and venial sin; plus that obligatory church attendance and the collection plate. Running counter to that is Eastern mysticism, featuring karma, reincarnation, austere disciplines, mantras, spinning prayer wheels, and the worship of seven-armed goddesses. I won't even go down the road to the extreme practices of Islam and the Hebrew traditions. Suffice it to say, very complicated!

Okay, now let's make this as simple and clean as possible. The Shift that is now happening has arranged life on Earth for the finders to the point of absolute simplicity. What could be more simple than this: Consciousness is all there is and *you are That.* There is no big father-God above, and you aren't a separate, lowly little worm down here trying to figure out how to appease this sometimes angry and judgmental Creator, or face the consequences of being doomed. There is only one energy pervading all realities.

After all, this energy, which we can call Consciousness or Source, is here for all eternity. One of the laws of the third dimension is "as above, so below." We humans prefer never to be bored here on Earth, right? Well, Source will never be bored either. So it pops into the world of appearance using mental energy that is much like a dream state, and it plays a game of "hide and seek" with itself that returns feedback on all aspects of knowing itself. To be really interesting, Source manifests every single individual within each species as a unique original, never before or ever again seen. This goes for all of creation, from snowflakes to humans. In this way, it avoids cloning identical experiences in its game of hide and seek.

It has certain experiences as minerals—say, as a mountain—and others as plants, insects, and animals. It has also developed a certain animal capable of the highest experience of all—the human animal with its discriminating mind and complex emotions.

Remember, Source wants to experience all possible scenarios in each and every species. The instincts, drives, yearnings, feelings, and emotions of the human animal are to be experienced, not repressed. No other species knows what it means to suppress what comes naturally, whether instinctual or emotional.

Let's come back to Occam's Razor now and consider the purpose of life. When, as seekers, we first asked ourselves, "Why am I here?" we were totally overwhelmed with contradictory answers from all sides. We heard:

- To evolve your consciousness
- To raise others' consciousness
- To be enlightened in this lifetime
- To help others
- To increase your virtues
- To rid yourself of vices
- To be responsible
- To make correct choices
- To obey the laws (all of them!)
- To appease God
- To be good (every day, in every way, I will try harder to be better!)

Trying to comply meant going to churches of various religions, therapists, self-help groups, and life-enhancement workshops for all of our seeking lives. And what did we have to show for all this intentional effort? The despair that leads to the dark night of the soul.

The only simple solution is as follows:

1. Realize that we are here to enjoy and accept our lives exactly as they are. Everything is exactly the way it

should be for a unique experience in your individual mind/body organism.

2. Accept that all our emotions—not just the positive ones—are meant to be experienced. Life is enriched exceedingly by all the negative emotions as well.

3. Just be! Do nothing as a spiritual goal! Understanding is all you need to go home in peace and freedom.

4. For understanding, reread points 1 to 3 above.

5. Consciousness is all there is. You are That! As infinite Intelligence dancing in the third dimension, you cannot make a mistake or screw up your destiny. Your destiny was already fulfilled the moment you showed up in a body. You are here as a vehicle for Source to experience this glorious third dimension and all the human predicaments that our emotions may produce.

6. You don't have to save or help anyone, including and especially yourself, and you couldn't even if you wanted to. You are henceforth absolved from being God's little helper.

Now if any of you seekers or finders out there reading this can possibly offer me a more simple solution than this, I would truly appreciate it. Otherwise, if this is the most simple one, then it must be the only true one, according to William of Occam.

chapter 5

The Greatest Secret
of the Shift

Perhaps you wonder why this particular book found its way to you. All the letters and e-mails received over the last two years regarding how *Onions* mysteriously and synchronistically found its way to seekers all over the globe would be great material for a book of its own. Copies have been left on airplane seats in Hong Kong or in remote parts of India. And sometimes as a result, surprised readers experienced and expressed their own awareness of the Shift. This chapter may well play a role of synchro-destiny in your Shift. I am about to share the most extraordinary secret of the whole spiritual quest and the key process in the Shift, one that to my knowledge has never before been discussed.

The way I see it, Source has very gradually and ever-so-subtly revealed itself to itself over millions of years of hide-and-seek play on this planet. Being born into the human predicament means that built right into your DNA is an automatic trigger called *the longing*. Up until now, this longing has just been a very vague desire to understand the thoughts of God and appease It. This started with cave dwellers attributing divine powers to forces they couldn't understand. Rituals and superstitions started around campfires and ended up as drawings on cave walls.

Then Source finally spoke publicly, as Moses, who led the Jews. Until now the longing to know God was not intense enough for most people to actually want to self-realize—they only wanted to avoid God's punishment. Then in A.D. 500, Buddha shared a message of compassion for all living things as part of our own energy. Mohammed then appeared with his message of mercy to all who have grieved us, since Allah is the One and only energy. Jesus came along and improved our understanding a little more by overruling the "eye for an eye" ethic; instead he recommended that you love your neighbor as yourself. Even more important was the clue that the Father and Jesus were one energy.

Do your see where this trend is headed? One by one, awakened ones came along through the ages to keep the clarification and the evolution of a consciousness moving in the direction of the big Shift that is occurring right now. Why didn't Source just come right out and reveal itself in full clarity and understanding at the very beginning? When I observe this long history, and the buildup of delicious anticipation that has been intensifying until now, I see how Source always seems to work by paradox: If you were going to unfold a grand plan with spectacular results, you would logically and conventionally design it to arrive with brilliant steps toward a certain conclusion. Now just follow the complete opposite of this human logic, and you'll see how the divine paradox of Source usually works.

Remember that Source is an eternal reality. Limited mind thinks: "Uh-oh, possible boredom here coping with eternity!" But the infinite Vastness of Source is playful and loves to amuse itself in ways that the finite human mind can never understand. So Source has been ever so slowly rolling back the veils of ignorance that were purposefully designed into the human predicament from the very beginning.

All of this is to say that the time has arrived in the history of humankind to crank up the intensity of this longing to know God until it's so high that it's unbearable—until the seekers do wake up and remember who they really are. Once you remember that you are the Consciousness that is all there is, everything else becomes so simple and clear that you never again need a teacher to explain spiritual realities to you.

I have to admit that as I was experiencing my own Shift, the contrast was so severe between what I was clearly seeing now with the veils of ignorance and forgetfulness removed, and what I had always been told by conventional, third-dimensional wisdom to be the truth, that the possibility of my having gone off the deep end of madness definitely loomed heavily in my imagination. How could something so mysterious and complicated as humanity's relationship to God suddenly be so clean, simple, and clear after millions of years of muddled superstition and intentional efforts to get there from here?

Wait, it gets better! What would you think now, after this long intro, if I told you that the deliverance, which is the actual key to processing your original wake-up call to the Shift, is cleverly concealed by Source in the form of daily contractions? A *contraction* is any emotional resistance—anything that says "No!" to the current situation, or maybe even "Hell, no!" Contractions, before and after your Shift, happen at least a dozen times a day. They are an integral part of Source's plan to know itself more fully. If our mind's main function was not to polarize every thought into opposite camps of desire and resistance, we wouldn't have the possibility of all those negative emotions that come from resistance. If we didn't have negative emotions to experience life, one half of Source's whole raison d'être—that is, to know itself by playing human—would be unavailable. Yet we all thought that negative emotions and their contractions were things to be gotten rid of, changed into positive ones, or at least improved upon.

What avatar ever told us that the secret of the Shift lies in a miraculous power to dance "yes" to the "no" of contraction? Yet it's true. This power is the Witness, who identifies not with the contraction, but with itself as the Consciousness who understands the function and role of all contractions.

One concept that almost always pops up at the weekend intensives is the expectation that as part of this Shift, one will gain supernatural abilities. Nothing fancy, just the usual ones of walking on water or through walls, curing cancers, and reading thoughts. Think about this for a moment: If these were indeed included in the Shift, would they give you one more iota of happiness, freedom, or fulfillment once the newness wore off? Of course not, because they are still directed by you as a product of your mind. They are outside of you. Your only center of happiness is in inside your ancient memory and understanding of who you are.

Now imagine the power of a miracle so great that humankind has never experienced it before. I'm sure that all awakened ones in the past must have known this, but conveniently forgot to mention it to a world that wasn't ripe enough yet to understand its full and miraculous scope.

Anytime a contraction hits, the full power of the mind immediately and automatically engages to dispel that unpleasant emotion. But in the Shift, the Witness comes to the forefront of awareness and overrides the "no" with a relaxed and amused "yes." This is a fourth-dimensional power unavailable to those with both feet still planted in the third dimension. The miracle of the Witness dancing "yes" to a "no" is the very key and secret to your happiness, to your deliverance into the realms of deeper understanding and memory of who you really are. Without constant contractions to bring you into the present moment, you would soon fall back into forgetfulness of who you are. You are Satchitananda, and dancing "yes" to your third-dimensional "no's" won't let you forget it!

Dancing "yes" to a "no" is the practical and natural outcome once a separated little "me" remembers that Consciousness is all there is, and *I am that!* Whatever is—just as it is—is exactly the way it is supposed to be. The miracle and secret of dancing "yes" to the natural "no" is a supernatural embrace of what is.

~€୨~

chapter 6

Mangoes and Enlightenment

Within the context of my own Shift, it occurred to me that my process was certainly not unique, as I found out once I was released from prison and began my Satsang tour around the world. In sharing my story with thousands of others, I found a lot of common ground. For example, I saw that all seekers have this longing to go home, which is so intense that it eventually brings them to a dark night of the soul. And where is home? Home is the oneness that we already are but still yearn for while in a body. Home is my original nature without the confusion of seeming separation. Home is the beauty, awe, and comfort of living in each moment, knowing that all is well and exactly as it is supposed to be, and nothing needs to be fixed or changed.

I found something out, which I now term my *ripe mango solution,* about tree-ripened seekers: Regardless of how much intentional effort they did or did not put into their attempts to find their way home, they eventually ripened and fell off the seeker tree right into the rapture of finally finding their true home. Now I am

very familiar with mangoes due to years spent at our retreat center in Costa Rica, which has many mango trees of different
species. At certain times of the year, very strong winds will come
up and try to blow those mangoes off the branches, but to no
avail. Those little mangoes just hang on for dear life and nothing
can shake them loose. But then comes a time of ripening when
they are so affected by their "shift" that the very day they are perfectly ripe, they just plop off the trees with no effort or shaking. A
day before this, they are still a little bitter. Two days later, they are
overripe. If any of you have ever seen mangoes get ripe all at once,
you understand the glazed-over eyes of us poor mango addicts who
can't get enough of this delicious fruit at a time like this.

My whole point here is that in our time, all the ripe seekers
are falling off their "spiritual trips" and just relaxing into the
knowledge that all is well in this life, exactly as is! Why now?
Because it is time. Because a Shift is happening at last. Right
now! Without effort!

However, there was a part of my own Shift that was amusing
in the sense that I had no clue about its reality before it happened.
It had to do with spiritual understanding about the balance and
contrast in Source's dance in this world of appearance.

My understanding and knowing at a level beyond the mind
that Consciousness is all there is came with a clarity about how
Consciousness plays in the third dimension. I am not implying
that this has never been said before. It's just that I had never
heard this in all my years of intense spiritual disciplines and
research. And it came through me with absolutely no question or
doubt about its authenticity.

So when I explained it to those participating in my intensives, I was amazed that a sea of heads were nodding in total
agreement as though this were the most natural description one
could make about Source.

It goes like this: Source, like all energy, pulses every so often
from a state of rest into a universe of appearance. At rest there is

only infinite expansion and pure Potential, but no limitation. There, Source experiences its own Nature or Essence as Satchitananda. Would it be fair to say that this is the positive side of its true Nature? As soon as Source enters the world of appearance, duality exists due to the mere definition of the limitation involved in every aspect of the third dimension. The opposite of positive is the shadow side of its Nature. At rest Source fully experiences only the positive aspects of Satchitananda, but what about a full experience, one that also includes negativity? What, to quote *Star Wars,* does the "dark side of the Force" feel like?

Remember, we are talking about an energy here that while at rest is totally impersonal. The only way to have a personal experience is to limit that infinite expansion into a mind/body organism. Yet even though the entire third dimension is the one energy or Consciousness of Source, there is still no personal energy that is directing traffic here, no big-white-Father-in-the-sky concept that you grew up with, who says: "Okay, you over there get to be enlightened, but you with the beard don't! You get the promotion at work, and your buddy there gets fired! Joel gets a soulmate to live with, and Sally has to live alone!"

It's not like that. Source has arranged everything in the third dimension to function on autopilot, with maximum efficiency, without personal supervision, and within the framework of infinite intelligence.

I actually overheard a conversation of Source with itself regarding this matter:

> Well, it's that time again to end this rest period and plunge back into the world of appearance to liven things up a bit. I feel like exploring the shadow side this time of my positive, loving, aware, and blissful Nature. It's time to create another universe and live again as a man so I can get the full range of emotions. I would like to make sure that this situation is supermaximum, but without it getting out of control on the extremes.
>
> Let's make sure that every time a human life is experi-

enced, it will be a totally new and different sensation from any other life experience I ever had or might have in the future. Let's keep it in perfect balance as far as the freedom and limitation allowed within that lifetime. This way no life will be any better or worse than any other life ever lived. Each one, though, will be absolutely unique because each will have a unique DNA strand with all the predispositions built in. A unique conditioning will then further differentiate each, and that programming will come from their family and cultural upbringing.

From my infinite intelligence there will be a godzillion different lives lived that will then give me the whole enchilada of what it feels like to limit this Infinite Potential in the world of appearance.

To make sure that all is experienced, we will have a law not only of supreme balance between the freedom and limitation parts, but also of contrast. Whatever is experienced in one way over here, the opposite contrast will also be felt over there. Even within a single lifetime, sooner or later a contrast will always show up to balance out the experience of what has preceded it. Even every word that is uttered while in a human body will be a concept that springs from the duality and limitation of the mind, so that the very opposite of that concept is also equally true and valid. Every emotion in every person will be experienced from both sides.

If we are going to have goodness, then we must also have to know evil. Joy will be contrasted by sorrow. Healthy people will have to know sickness, and life will have to be contrasted in the end by death. Not just by some of my appearances, but all of them!

To assure a constant, nonstop flow of emotions, everyone will get a mind that interprets every thought that it receives into a polarity of "for" and "against." This will set up desire for, and resistance against, what the mind judges as good or bad. The desire and resistance will then set up expectations, which will always result in disappointment, no matter what the content. While this may be interpreted as suffering and sorrow, it does assure that the shadow side of Satchitananda will also be explored.

No emotion is to be left unturned or untouched. But always done so in a manner that every life lived has an even balance, in the final analysis, of the freedom and limitation that both the positive and negative emotions contain.

What makes this so meaningful in the Shift is that we finally understand the ramifications involved in our reality of life just as it is. We realize we are Consciousness Itself having these life experiences, and that all is going perfectly well according to divine design. Therefore, we no longer have any need to control our negative emotions by either repressing them or acting them out. We can just Witness them, not identifying with them as being in any way contrary to what is "supposed" to be, but observing that they are mere variations on the soap opera that this third dimension really is.

We come to realize that we are most divine when we are being most human in our frailties. For this human experience to be maximally effective, it must be felt as real. When passions are hot, they don't feel like "just some ole illusion," or the maya conventionally emphasized by Eastern spirituality.

Are you feeling anger, rage, envy, jealousy, lust, or depression? Good! That's just part of why we are here. What to do about these demons? Nothing! Just sit and observe as they happen, instead of trying to make them go away or get better. Suddenly you also observe yourself dancing "yes" to the big "no" of daily contractions. And this, my fellow dancers, is called the big Shift to the fourth dimension. You don't necessarily get any "better." Your perception of reality just Shifts to that of a Witness in choiceless awareness. You have already spent a lifetime being a spiritual warrior trying to control your destiny according to the concepts of each moment. Enough is enough already!

chapter 7

~~~~

The Satsang Circle

The old spiritual paradigm dictated that if you were a seeker, in touch with the longing to self-realize and go home, then you would seek out a guru or teacher and dedicate yourself to austere spiritual disciplines under his/her direction in this quest.

This probably worked for one in a million seekers. Definitely not fun!

I see a new paradigm ushered in by the enormous Shift of energy that is available in this new millennium. For whatever reason, Source is now playing with a new experience in the third dimension. *All* seekers are finally heading home, instead of just a few awakened ones here and there. No more gurus or avatars are required to spearhead the Shift.

Instead it will facilitate the one percent of the world that is now consciously in touch with a longing that Source has cranked up to such intensity that it can no longer be ignored, using a most simple, playful, and ingenious process. As I see it, this new paradigm is the Satsang circle.

This book is a perfect place to focus on how to realize a Satsang circle in your area of the planet. Keep in mind that Satsang is the most powerful demonstration of the fourth dimension that I know of. The power of the sun pales in comparison.

Sixty million people are not going to be visited by any other guru in this Shift except the Satsang circle. It has always been said that when the student is ready, the master will appear. Well, here we are!

And here comes the Satsang circle.

I could not be so enthusiastic and confident about the power of Satsang to move seekers into the fourth dimension if I didn't see it at work in a different city every single weekend, in a new Satsang circle. The response is unanimous. The Shift is definitely felt. And Satsang is the only facilitator as far as I am concerned. Why is the power of Satsang such a well-kept secret for so many thousands of years?

Didn't Jesus give us a pretty strong hint when he promised that when two or more were gathered in his name that He (the power of Satsang/Divine Wisdom/Inner Guidance) would be right there in the middle?

Source seems to be going through a lot of machinations here and now to initiate a millennial Shift. You are being detached from a lifelong sense of identity of who you thought you were, accompanied by a sense of loss that I call the dark night of the soul. That poor body of yours is being rewired to handle the higher frequency of the Shift that, meanwhile, results in general malaise, chronic fatigue, and even nervous breakdown. But on the brighter side, here comes your closest ally, your best friend, and your new spiritual teacher: Satsang!

Satsang is an ancient Sanskrit word that means both "holy company" and "discourse of truth." Satsang happens infallibly when two or more seekers gather to share their "sacred truth." What is a sacred truth other than anything that comes out of your mouth or heart in this situation!

There is far too much hype in modern times that leaves many waiting breathlessly for a new avatar to usher in the millennium with a new teaching of enlightenment. The Buddhist tradition has always said that this avatar's name would be Maitreya. Well, where is he? Actually, Maitreya is already here—you see, *Maitreya* means "my friend" in Sanskrit. And that is how this Shift from seeker to finder will happen. Friends will share their sacred truths with friends in Satsang circles.

Every city housing seekers will develop Satsang circles to spread the good news. Back in 1978, when I first got hold of the Ecstasy pill, I couldn't pay people to try it. But a few friends shared some with their inner circles, and in a few years Ecstasy was spread all over the globe. That's the principle of the Satsang circle.

So let me share from my weekly intensives what really affects the power of the Satsang circle.

Attitude

Enter the circle with an open heart. There are no answers that the mind can understand to explain the Vastness. Previously we thought we knew how to get from here to there. Now we know only one thing for sure: We don't know squat!

Look around at the faces of your participating circle. See in each and every mind/body organism an appearance of Source. "Consciousness is all there is, and *I am That,* and so is everyone else in this room!"

Every time someone opens their mouth, pure sacred truth comes out, no matter what the word forms sound like. The words don't matter! Satsang works not because of any words, but in spite of them. Satsang's power comes from the transmission of energy that results when you come together to experience your own sacred truth, regardless of whether words are even spoken at all.

Satsang has no agenda. We are not here to convince anyone of our own extremely unique experience and truth. We are here to share the power of a quantum leap of energy and wisdom that results automatically when a Satsang circle is formed.

Satsang is not in session to solve anyone's particular problems or give anyone advice. We may share our contractions with the circle, but that is part of the process. The answers all come from within, not from without.

One key word to keep in mind about attitude is *respect*. When someone is sharing an experience with the circle, please don't interrupt until that person is through with their comments. This is not a discussion or support group. Pure magic always happens in Satsang because all the power of the Universe is present and available at the intuitive level when the heart is open. If the mind could have solved all our third-dimensional stories with words, it already would have done so eons ago. The mind and words can't deliver! Satsang always does—without words!

The power of Silence is part of Satsang's magic. If there are pauses and spaces in your sharing with each other, relish the silence as even more powerful than the words. Because we still have a foot solidly planted in the third dimension, we will always need to use words in our sharings. But the Silence inevitably shows up in Satsang. When it does, welcome it as your best connection to the power of Satsang.

Protocol Guidelines

1. Each Satsang circle has a person designated to interface with the New Freedom Press home office for support materials and updates.

2. Rotate the meeting sites, usually someone's home, unless the circle is held regularly at a public facility.

3. Rotate the facilitators. Experience has shown that if only one person is the facilitator and the circle is always held at their home, and that person later drops out, then the group usually disbands instead of regrouping. Human nature!

4. Agree on the starting time and length of the circle, usually between one and two hours, and honor the agreement.

5. Typically a Satsang circle will start off in silence/meditation for 15 to 20 minutes. Next we play music, such as Peter Makena's awakened compositions, or a short Satsang video or audiocassette to prime the sharing with words. Finally, we share open, loving Satsang and end with another ten minutes or so of silence.

6. If you keep in mind that the content of the words doesn't really matter, then an example of what you can share is:

   - your own individual experience of the Shift;
   - the human predicament;
   - the nature of your contractions;
   - your own unique brand of deliverance;
   - a poem (yours or someone else's);
   - a song;
   - short writings that may have inspired you;
   - a joke;
   - a piece on a musical instrument; or
   - last, but definitely not least, silence.

During weekend intensives, we play with a pet-peeve list and use the statements from *Onions'* chapter titled "Are We Having Fun Yet?" as a method to start everyone sharing Satsang, so they can experience the magic for themselves and thereby touch everyone with their "words." No matter what words may come out of your mouth, you will affect and transmit high-frequency energy to everyone in the circle when your heart is open.

7. Agree to follow the protocol, and be clear about it with new participants as they join your circle.

8. If you wish that something you share with the circle should remain confidential, inform the participants.

Support from New Freedom Press

We will start off your Satsang circle with a kit that includes videos and audios. We will then continue to provide new ones as ticklers for priming the inspiration pump. You may connect with other Satsang circles through our bulletin board on the Internet at **www.SatyamNadeen.com.** If my original vision is holding true, then I definitely see these Satsang circles sweeping the planet with light and wisdom to facilitate the Shift that all seekers are going through. This is my greatest message to you, way beyond the words of a book or intensive.

Satsang is where you will find your greatest joy, wisdom, inspiration, and understanding of the most incredible phenomenon that has ever happened in the history of the planet, a Shift from the third dimension to the fourth while still in a body.

If you feel inspired to be the initial facilitator for a group in your area, please contact our office to get you started. As readers from your area send in coupons from *Onions* to connect to us, we will forward their names to you as a possible Satsang circle participant. If your area grows enough to sponsor an intensive, I will come to participate with you.

chapter 8

Does Anyone Really Know What Enlightenment Is?

Of all the possible topics in the realms of spirituality, this is by far the most confusing one I have ever come across. *Enlightenment* generally refers to living in a state of awakened, cosmic consciousness; to oneness, freedom, fulfillment, self-realization, and so on.

What I mean by enlightenment is that a person has gradually, or sometimes suddenly, remembered who they are at their core essence. The ancient memory that Consciousness is all there is, and *I am That* comes from a forgotten, deeply hidden place in our own consciousness. Once the first glimpse of this comes to the foreground of memory, a slight Shift in the perception of reality starts to affect our daily lives. The big illusion that we have free will and choice—that we are "the doer"—fades away as the glimpses get longer and more frequent. Eventually we are swept away into the rapture of total freedom that is always provided by knowing who you are.

In Satsang, I try to stay away from using the word *enlightenment*. I prefer to use the word *Shift* to prevent the confusion that's been caused by 5,000 years of building the "E word" into a giant, unfathomable myth.

I call it a Shift because that's what really happens.

A person enters the world as Source in appearance. However, the game plan set up by Infinite Intelligence is that we enter a body in a state of forgetfulness of who we really are. We think that in the third-dimensional world, we are the "doers" of our destiny. This idea of "doing" then creates all the negative emotions that naturally flow from the disappointments set up by expectations in the first place. This is as it should be. The whole purpose of life in the third dimension is to know ourselves fully, and that includes the shadow side of the Source, once we find ourselves located in a dimension of duality and polar opposites, as is the case in the third dimension.

Under normal circumstances, a person will trip along for an average of some 70 years without ever having a clue that they are One with the energy that is the Source of all seen and unseen realities. Then they die. Then comes the big "Ah-ha!" experience of their whole life. Source has been playing hide and seek with itself for a whole lifetime—and now, at the moment of passing, we suddenly realize that we are not the lowly, limited, powerless, separated little being that we always thought we were. In a flash Source has found itself and obviously loves this experience of finding after a lifetime of confusion and seeking for the very meaning of life itself.

Now that's the normal pattern. We all know that no one has ever come back from an actual death. Not a *near*-death experience, mind you, but one in which their body actually decayed, and then told us about this "Ah-ha!" experience. So I had to use my own inner Wisdom and vision, which showed me all this quite clearly in my own Shift.

As far as we know from recorded history, a Shift of this magnitude has never happened before. Instead of sleepwalking through this whole life, then waking up and remembering our true nature and identity only at the moment of death, a multitude of seekers are actually remembering this while still alive and functioning in a body. Who are the seekers?

They are those of us who are consciously aware now and have been for most of this lifetime that we have a deep longing and yearning to "go home" and know the thoughts of God. We feel as if we ended up on the wrong planet by some huge cosmic mistake in the shipping department. What drives and motivates the other 99 percent of the population—things such as normal family life, careers with eight-to-five jobs, social and recreational activities, and the like—don't give enough juice to fulfill us. We crave something more. We don't even know what it is exactly that we need, but it has something to do with God and our interactive relationship therein.

Now out of the blue comes some new kind of cosmic energy field that changes our perception of everything that used to get us through this third dimension. First of all, our longing has been cranked up to maximum intensity. Nothing satisfies us now but a movement toward oneness. We get precipitated into a rather long period that I call *the dark night of the soul*. While languishing there our bodies seem to be undergoing some kind of electrical rewiring to handle the higher frequency of the Shift.

Then comes the first glimpses of the Shift in the subtle memories of who we are. They come and we think, *Ah, now I am in the Shift into the fourth dimension that Nadeen is talking about,* but then they vanish, leaving us depressed and disappointed once more. But then they return, and this time the glimpse is longer and deeper than before, only to slip away once more. This Shift becomes a bobbing in and out of the fourth dimension for at least two years or much longer, before it begins to stabilize into a permanent state of absolutely knowing and understanding that

Consciousness is all there is and I am That. The really big Shift is evident when you understand: Not only am I That, but everyone is also That. And that is far from the normal state of affairs on Earth here, as Jean-Paul Sartre so aptly summed up by saying, "Hell is other people!"

Contrary to conventional wisdom, enlightenment is not an act—it's not St. Paul getting knocked off his horse by lightning, as mentioned in the New Testament. You are not suddenly and fully Shifted into a new dimension of perception and awareness. Not even close! Does the sun like to just pop up from the horizon and show up overhead in a flash? Nature likes to take it slow and easy in its unfoldment. After all, we have all eternity at our disposal.

Get used to the idea that if you are reading this book, you are definitely a seeker. If so, then you are already involved deeply in this big Shift I keep talking about. The Shift has nothing to do with all the concepts you always imagined might happen around the idea of someone waking up while still in a body. It's so subtle and gradual that your closest friends and family are not even aware that you are changing so dramatically. *You* may not even realize how drastically your perception of reality is Shifting. It's almost never sudden or permanent at the git-go. It generally takes a dark night of the soul, a rewiring of your whole electrical energy grid, and a few years of deliverance. Then you can stand up before a whole circle of Satsang participants and say with total knowing and confidence: "*I am That,* and this understanding has propelled every aspect of my life into a dimension of new and total freedom."

chapter 9

The Myth of
Enlightenment

Whatever you thought you knew about enlightenment before
you read this book—that is, if you are a seeker like most—
is probably more myth than reality. And this is a barrier to the full
enjoyment of your newfound freedom as you move through the
stages of the Shift.

When my own Shift was happening, I didn't have a clue that
I would be calling it an awakening five years later in a book and
on a Satsang tour. At the time it just didn't fit any of the illusion-
ary niches in my former concepts about what enlightenment is
supposed to mean. Then I had the joy and privilege to interact
with over 10,000 seekers in their Shifts after my release from
prison. During the weekend intensives, there is a slot for sharing
what you always believed enlightenment is supposed to mean, or
at least hoped that it would mean for you someday. We laughed

till we cried as we spun out our fantasy concepts in front of the group. However, not all were laughing. Some were still grimly holding on for dear life in some kind of wishful thinking that they might still come true. But in every intensive, there have been too many seekers present who were actually far enough through the Shift to now consider themselves finders. And they would always set the record straight! These old, tired concepts just didn't stand a chance in the face of so much authentic experience being shared regarding what this Shift is all about. Satsang doesn't deal with theory. It deals with the actual experience of each participant sharing their lifelong adventure—first as a weary, discouraged seeker, and then as a relieved and joyful finder who can now describe from experience the freedom they are living.

In the pages that follow, I am going to outline some of the myths about enlightenment we deal with, and then present the actual reality of that myth in the context of this Shift. As far as I know, this may be the first time in print that this has been discussed. The myths are just nice concepts that may have been around for millennia. The realities are actual experiences of seekers who became finders due to the force field of this new energy.

chapter 10

Myth: Enlightenment Is a Peak Experience

If you are aware of the tantric approach to spiritual sexuality, then you are familiar with the term "peak orgasm." It comes and goes very quickly. What tantric yogis are looking for in their practice are "valley orgasms" that build very slowly, never "come," and stay within the framework of an enjoyable experience for countless hours.

This same parallel is applicable to the myth of enlightenment. I remember reading my first real introduction to these various states of so-called Cosmic Consciousness by Dr. R. M. Bucke back in the early 1960s. When he was describing his version of enlightenment in all these special people over the ages, he really only focused on what emerged as peak experiences, which in my experience of the Shift, are *not* "it." Peak experiences have the following qualities:

1. A peak experience is one that you might call mystical; it comes and goes by its own totally unpredictable timing. You can't just call it up with grace like you can dropping acid and then waiting an hour.

2. The peak experiences I hear about in every intensive are full of insights, feelings of love or oneness, maybe even some compassion, and then they are gone with the wind, and the confused seeker is left wondering where that feeling came from and why it had to go. In other words, the experience is connected to thoughts and emotions.

3. These peak experiences feel so clear and overwhelming when present, but quickly slip into a spacey, undefined, vague memory the minute you try to describe them to a friend or even yourself. You know the routine if you ever experimented with a mind-altering drug. It goes almost in an instant from the greatest insight of your whole life to "Now what was that great idea all about, anyway?"

4. It comes! It goes! It never lasts! The biggest letdown is that for however long they last—a moment, a day, maybe even two weeks—the seeker is totally convinced that they are now, finally, a finder, even an awakened one, and that this blissful state will never go away again. But it always does! And this is not the Shift!

   A peak experience is etched in time; for instance, you might think you had your first wake-up call on August 16, 1995, from 6:30 A.M. to 2:10 P.M. And then you lost it! Oh, the ecstasy of insight and the agony of landing back in the third dimension again. Well, that's how it goes with peak mystical experiences. You measure the degree of disappointment you will feel later by the exact inverse ratio of excitement you had at the peak. It's one of the laws of energy! You bob into a fourth-dimensional awareness for a while and bob back into the third again.

Reality: Aim Not for the Peak, but the Valley

The Shift that I am describing has nothing to do with the above qualities. It is much more akin to that of the tantric valley experience, except that at some point it becomes a permanent way of perceiving the play of Consciousness in this world of appearance. It has the following qualities:

1. The Shifted awareness is there to dive into at will, whenever! Think of a fish made out of water swimming in a sea of water who is completely aware that it is the same as what it is swimming in. Now see that the water is Consciousness. That's all there is! Only Consciousness! You do not have to sit in zazen meditation, breathing deeply and slowly for 11 hours, to encourage this awareness. You already are it, and it is always available to relax consciously into whenever you like. All I have to do is be silent for a moment and then ask, "Who is it right now that is aware of this silence?"

2. This valley experience is a no-brainer, not connected to any specific feelings. I walk around in the midst of chaos and seeming disorder and know instinctively, intuitively, at the core of my essence, that all is well! No thoughts about it, no overwhelming rush of emotions about it. Just a gentle, loving gratitude that is always present because Consciousness is all there is, and I am That.

3. You move from the vagueness of a peak experience; to the knowing beyond mind, beyond experience, beyond doubt, and beyond any question; into the peaceful valley of experience of the Shift. What do you know so clearly? You know who you are at a level that consumes the normal judging and doing motions of the active mind. No matter what you see out there through these new eyes of Source, you can't screw up or make a mistake in life. You are now a peaceful person living in a peaceful universe that you know is actually "perfect" and no longer needs you as God's little helper to fix it up.

4. The reality of the Shift urges you toward a level of awareness that never, ever goes away. And I like to call this awareness the Witness, because everyone can relate to it as a word and as an experience.

    When you were a small child, you heard your Witness speak to you, and you listened. Then the mind grew strong and dominated your life, as it is supposed to in the third dimension. After a lifetime of futile seeking, followed by a dark night of the soul, the Shift begins when the Witness comes back into the forefront of your awareness. Your identity gradually, subtly Shifts from that a of a mind-dominated person to that of the Witness watching all that is happening around it without identifying with any of it as being an integral part of itself. The Witness begins to dialogue in Satsang with the mind part of itself and gradually take over its control of awareness.

When you are Shifted, the Witness never forgets that it is Consciousness Itself. Whatever maelstrom of contractions may happen to be swirling around it, all is well and part of the play of Consciousness in this world of appearance. There's no need at all for the limited mind to understand the "why" of it all. Amazingly enough, the mind goes along peacefully in the clarity and knowingness of the Witness. Once you know you are the Witness and not the doer, you are living within the valley experience of the Shift.

chapter 11

Myth:
Enlightenment Is Bliss

The most common expectation I hear about at my intensives is that enlightenment will equal bliss. This is universally expected of enlightenment, and no other expectation is so highly esteemed. Maybe that is because the deepest driving force behind the human predicament is the need to be happy. To complicate it even further, the ancients who wrote the Upanishads and Vedas defined the very nature of Source as Satchitananda, which, as we discussed in chapter 2, translates from the ancient Sanskrit as "an eternal reality (Sat), in pure awareness (Chit), and *in bliss* (Ananda)." And so we expect that when we realize who we really are, we will be *in bliss,* also, because we are supposed to, right?

I am no scholar of Sanskrit, but I do know what this Shift feels like, and I am experiencing my own true nature, albeit in limited fashion—but I would not choose to use that word *bliss* as an accurate description of this permanent Knowingness of who I am. Yes, I have experienced bliss many, many times now in the Shift, but it is a peak experience. It comes and goes! What we are interested in here is what enlightenment really means. We have to investigate the valley experience that is always present and doesn't slip away from us on a chance wind.

My experience of bliss is that when it is present, it renders me almost dysfunctional, it never lasts more than 30 minutes, and it is present without any cause I can connect it to. Then it's gone! And I'm left wondering: "What just happened?" Surely a bliss that comes and goes cannot be the essence of the awakening or remembering of who we really are. However, bliss definitely does seem to hang around the periphery of this Shift. Finders in the Shift all report a bout of it now and then. But no one is saying that they live in bliss as a constant state of awareness. To my knowledge, no one in recorded history has ever even intimated that this is the case.

Yet, bliss is still the number-one box office attraction, the most coveted prize of enlightenment. Just wait till the seekers find out that a deep peace that lasts and lasts is infinitely better than a bliss that comes and goes.

Reality: The True Essence of the Shift Lies Not in Bliss, but in Presence

The third dimension springs from the function of the mind and is experienced as separation. However, the fourth dimension of pure creative Spirit witnesses itself and the whole third dimension in pure choiceless awareness, unconditional love, stillness, and a peaceful joy not connected to any specifics. How do I know this? Because that is my experience most of the time when I'm not in the middle of a contraction. I call this witnessing Presence. This is the real meaning and unfoldment of enlightenment.

So far, I have been leading up to this great secret, which is deeply hidden from the rampant concepts surrounding enlightenment: The Shift involves the emergence of the Witness from the background of your awareness to the forefront. And just what does this Witness observe? I call it Presence.

The Shift is a bridge between the eternal Oneness and our illusory sense of separation. This bridge leads to Presence. Presence is who we are at our core essence, but it is constantly interrupted by the mind making judgments, resisting, expecting, and interpreting all sensory input as duality and polarity. Before the Shift, we are never at home—always out to lunch. Then we find Presence! Finding Presence is no big secret. It is always here in the present moment. It hangs out in the spontaneous aliveness of the unknown, beyond the limits of our conditioning and pre-dispositions. But only here in Presence is the awareness of what truly is, and that frees us from the false image of separated self.

Presence and the *Witness* are synonyms in the vocabulary of the Shift. The mind creates an illusion of separation. Then there is this Shift, and our new identity is no longer connected to or dominated by a mind that can only judge. Now, as if by magic, we are with the Witness, who we truly are, observing whatever truly is, in choiceless awareness. This act of witnessing—which never comes and goes and is always present—is what I call Presence.

As the Witness we are not passive. We live in passionate, active acceptance of what truly is, while releasing everything else the mind may present to the wonder of this glorious, be-here-now moment. Suddenly we discover, in this release, that as the Witness we are actually the one and only Source of all there is.

Presence is a space that is so open, so aware, so welcoming of what is that it would never occur to the Witness to change or fix anything. It is all so perfect already—just the way it is—just the way it is supposed to be!—in spite of the alternatives offered by the mind from its imperfect viewpoint. The Witness watches the mind run off in a flurry of options and understands that this is what good little minds are designed to do. But if you don't identify with it, you are free of it, even in the midst of it.

There is a Witness who is aware, and then there are objects that the Witness observes, such as:

- warm sunshine
- a knot of fear in your gut
- the smell of hot coffee in the morning
- a huge contraction of impatience while stuck in traffic

Now there is a letting-go even of one who is aware, and all that remains is *Presence Itself.* You may have no idea of how delicious this awareness is of just being, doing nothing, understanding everything, and free of all need to struggle or engage in any intentional effort to live this life "right." Life just lives itself through you, and you are the Witness of it, lost in Presence, observing it all in the present moment.

But you can't "do" Presence, because you *are* Presence. How could you practice, as you do yoga or meditation, something that you already are? Presence is totally effortless and nearer to you than your own breathing. All that happens is that we recognize the Witness, and Presence naturally occurs. The mind's function is to interpret this process, but the identity with the Witness overrides this sidestep. In the cosmic game of hide and seek, Source has found itself in Presence while still in a limited mind and body.

Presence contains within it a kind of override of the normal functions of our minds to judge, fix, or become. It overrides the feeling of separation, the identity with the little "me" that can only live in the past or future and doesn't have a clue about the awareness of the present moment.

When Presence is experienced by the Witness, we are suddenly comfortable in a realm where the future is always unknown. We are free of the mind's need for certainty and assurances that we won't be annihilated someday. We can already feel our eternalness growing as the dream of a limited individuality slowly dies.

Presence is the *Knowingness* that we are not just a fraction of the whole, but the Source of the whole. Presence reveals the oneness and discovery of who we really are. It's an end to the confusion of the human predicament and a freedom from the need to become and do. Presence is the secret of finally knowing you are home for good.

Enlightenment means light entering the darkness, and presence is that which blows away the illusions and concepts that kept us trapped in the darkness. How simple presence is! It just sees what is, as is.

With what is the Witness present? With whatever is happening, whether the pleasant taste of good food, the unpleasantness of self-judgment, or the ambiguous feeling of just being present, not productive and useful. Presence shines on all that is happening and knows that all is well. We can't direct Presence to any particular aspect of our soap opera because that would interrupt the flow and would be directed by the mind rather than by the Witness.

Presence is just shining on *all* of life as our infinite, innate wisdom presents it to use. Presence is not a tool—not some kind of spiritual discipline. It is all-encompassing and serves as its own reward. Presence is the overall relaxing into the active embrace of life as it is, and as it presents itself. Presence is beyond questions, doubts, and striving. The mind goes on override, the breathing evens out, the body is relaxed, and the view looking out over the third dimension through the eyes of Source is truly well and cosmic! My senses are more alive than ever before. All of a sudden I am touching, tasting, smelling, and hearing for the first time in a way that is so fresh and original. I am now the Witness living in Presence, in my original innocence finally regained. Life is now real, passionately alive, and I no longer have to fix it. Just bask in it as it unfolds. With even a little hint of bliss now and then to keep it interesting.

chapter 12

Myth: Enlightenment
Comes Through a Guru
and Spiritual Disciplines

This whole idea of striving toward enlightenment has been with us for many thousands of years. It was mostly confined to the East, principally India and Tibet, but then moved out to China and Japan as well. What we have inherited from this tradition is a strong set of concepts surrounding the role of a teacher and the need for ascetic spiritual practices to somehow force this lifting of the veils of forgetfulness.

There are several fatal flaws in this approach. We begin by understanding that Source is here in the world of appearance playing hide and seek, discovering its true identity while lost in the limitation and duality of the mind. What I have observed is that very gradually, much like the almost-imperceptible movement of the sun from the morning horizon to the full overhead position at noon, so has this game of gradually revealing Itself to Itself progressed over the millennia.

Source would now and then draw from its laws of contrast and paradox to wake up one out of a hundred million people, just to keep the hope of enlightenment alive and juicy. Someone like Buddha would come along with a strong longing to find his way home, follow all the known spiritual disciplines of the day, and wake up—not because of them, but in spite of them after he saw the futility of intentional effort. Buddha had no guru. After half a lifetime of living in the freedom of knowing his true identity, he was party to a book of 10,000 do's and don'ts, rules and regulations of how to get and maintain enlightenment. What a paradox, but that's how Source loves to amuse itself!

In the West we cherish Jesus, who also woke up without a guru and not necessarily devoted to any harsh disciplines. After his departure, the Catholic Church created enough dogma, canonical law, precepts, virtues, and vices to drive anyone nuts who really believes that they speak for God!

What I am driving at is that whenever we had an awakened teacher or avatar come along, it was always the exception to the rule and never the normal result of following a guru and his recommended practices.

Three parts of this equation don't work. First, the student: The general movement in spiritual striving is from separation to oneness. One of the forces driving the human predicament in the third dimension is the need to be "special" in every possible way. Your car, family, guru, and even your dog needs to be special. We hope that if we are special, we will fill the bottomless pit of anxiety that our sense of separation is constantly stoking.

But one of the great aspects of the Shift is that you transcend the need to be special and get to feel how delicious it is to just be ordinary for the first time in your life. And so the myth of the need for a teacher is exposed here, because we especially need our teacher/guru to be very *very* special—and that just causes more separation, instead of the oneness we are looking for.

Second, you have the problem of the teacher/guru dealing with all these devotees and their adulation, which contaminates by mere osmosis what started out as their own awakening and the fresh discovery of just being ordinary. With growing devotees, adulation, power, and time, you eventually see a crash and burn of any guru on a pedestal. The new law of the fourth dimension: You get to be ordinary, and no one is special.

Now we come to the third and final problem with trying to become enlightened by following a guru. Let's start with the most sacred cow of all disciplines, the sine qua non of awakening techniques—meditation. Reality byte: To engage in any technique such as meditation, you must become a "doer," someone who thinks they have to get from here to there. Basically a confused, ignorant human who believes that by some magic technique or ritual they can arrive at a divine nature and escape the human predicament, simply by controlling or stopping the mind with some meditative technique. After all, it sure feels like the mind is the cause of all this suffering, so why not fix it through meditation? Forget about the fact that the mind is just functioning normally by judging and dividing every thought into polarity.

All sense of spiritual doing moves you eventually to a state of despair over the results you would like. All spiritual disciplines are doing, so they belong in the category of myth.

Reality: *There Are No Gurus, Teachers, or Special Techniques That Can Speed Up Your Personal Shift*

The above statement directly challenges at least 5,000 years of sacred spiritual traditions, but if the Source is to fully reveal Itself to Itself, then all the old distortions, half-truths, and myths have to be cleared out right now. No more secrets! Not in politics, religions, or relationships—and certainly not regarding the Shift!

Each and every one of us is equally Source. No one has more divinity, more wisdom, more essence of Source than anyone or anything else. If we are not Shifted yet, then it isn't time for that yet. If someone else is awake and remembers their true identity, they can transmit nothing by intentional effort that will wake you up.

Each and every person in the universe has a completely unique genetic set of predispositions and conditioning. When one wakes up and calls oneself a guru, that person can only describe their own unique experience—they cannot prescribe what will work for you, or how you will actually experience the Shift, except for some generalities. Source loves diversity and doesn't ever clone experiences—not even the Shifted awareness kind.

Your guru, in case you are still looking for one, lives within you, has always been there, and will emerge as the Witness once your own Shift begins. You can't summon up the Witness by dancing impatiently around the flagpole of your longing. The Witness emerges at the forefront of your awareness just as the ripe mango falls off the tree. Remember what I said about the futility of trying to shake those green mangoes off before they are ripe?

The only guru you will ever need is the infinite wisdom of Satguru, who is your own true nature, your essence, and your new identity someday soon.

Just to add a little humorous gossip to this whole frenzied guru scene, in my own travels around the world on a Satsang tour, I have observed the following: Those seekers who are still hanging on to the person of any guru, living or dead, still keeping them up there on a pedestal, are not yet fully engaged in the Shift. I would definitely state from observing them that hanging on to a guru is a fatal occupational hazard of any seeker who wants to totally and permanently Shift to a finder. The devotees I meet who are hanging out at the master's feet or in his old ashram are on the outside looking in. However, I do know, also from experience, that when their time is ripe, they will leave the master with loving gratitude in their hearts, and move on *alone* into the dark night of the soul, and from there into the rapture of the Shift. I sure wish I could say that I have found exceptions to this observation, but none as yet.

As far as the myth surrounding spiritual disciplines, just know this: There is absolutely nothing you can do to speed up your own Shift. First of all, there isn't anything in the entire third dimension that isn't spiritual. If you are Source in appearance, then watching football on TV is as "spiritual" as meditating in the middle of your candles and incense. *There is nothing to do! Just be! Understanding is all!*

Understanding and your Witness emerge when the time is ripe. If you are a seeker and in touch with your longing to go home, that time is right now, and you are already in process. Just relax into the "nondoing" attitude that will soon take over your whole life. If you want to play a bit while you are in the delivery room, go share Satsang with your friends. It never fails to lighten you up! Satsang is the only dance I know of that can offset the impatience of the mind and the intensity of the longing.

chapter 13

~∞~

Myth: Enlightenment Will Be the End of All My Troubles

This concept is right up there in popularity with the myth of neverending bliss. My opening statement about this is always the same: "There is *no practical advantage* to being totally awake, enlightened, or Shifted while still in the third dimension."

- Your bills are still overdue.
- You still don't meet your soulmate or twin flame, if you are looking for one.
- Your car still breaks down in rush hour in the only possible place without a shoulder to pull over.
- You still catch a cold twice a year.

- Your mother-in-law still nags you.

- Your home team still doesn't make it to the Super Bowl.

- You may never get that promotion at work.

This myth is the flip side of the desire for neverending bliss. We want to be happy. Not having troubles or worries might go a long way toward this. If we can't have neverending bliss, at least we could have no more problems in this life.

But did any saint or awakened master ever tell this to their followers? I don't think so! Their lives continued on with problems unabated, the same as everyone else's. Many people who have lived in the inner circles of the famous awakened masters, Osho and Papaji, have related in Satsang how these guys lived in contraction city, right up to the day they died. No one escapes the universal law of balance between freedom and limitation in this third dimension. Not before the Shift, not after.

No one who was truly awake ever said that life was a picnic after the wake-up. But in our need to be happy, we hope against hope that maybe this is "it." We start out early in life with sex, drugs, and rock and roll to see if that's where it is. After that burns out, we turn to more conventional wisdom such as marriage, raising a family, doing the career route—only to end up as lonely and empty as ever.

Then a curious things happens to about one percent of the population, whom I call seekers. A valve opens somewhere in their makeup, which says: When all else fails to make you happy and fulfilled, find out the thoughts of God. These people then substitute all previous desires for relationship, fortune, and fame for one of a burning desire to go home, which vaguely means interacting with the Divine instead of gross worldly energy.

But here we still have a separated seeker who believes they are the "doer." So they are still trying to make it happen! They check out every spiritual teacher who comes along, every new or ancient meditation technique, any and every self-improvement workshop available, and a monthly run to their local New Age bookstore to see if there are any hot new items there as a quick fix to their dilemma.

Reality: Welcome to the Dark Night of the Soul!

Not only does the Shift not fix all your little problems in life, but its path just happens to pass through the dark night of the soul. I wish I could tell you otherwise, that I have met at least one seeker turned finder who escaped this passageway to the fourth dimension. However, there is a natural order in the bleak chaos of this period.

Seekers have spent a lifetime being the "doer." This is as it should be, because part of our makeup is the driving force of a mind whose only function is to judge, fix, do, and make happen. Not only does the mind try to fix the whole third-dimensional world, but when it hears about a fourth-dimensional Shift into awakened awareness, it then tries to "do" this also. Our Witness, in its infinite wisdom, lets the mind run its natural, normal course until one day we begin to realize how futile and empty the results of a lifetime of seeking have been.

The Shift can only happen in quiet and solitude. However, it goes against the very nature of the mind to ever just be quiet and alone—hence, the wisdom of the dark night of the soul. We find ourselves feeling deep despair and abandonment, we notice our lackluster careers and relationships, and most of all, we feel that God has turned Its back to us. All this finally forces us to shut up, be still, and listen to the faint whispers of our Witness. It then begins to revive ancient memories of who we really are.

The dark night of the soul seems to be the most efficient way for the Witness to capture our full attention and baffle the mind's attempts to do or fix life. Once we wake up and remember who we are, the next big myth-breaker evolves. Not only are these contractions or daily "troubles" not going to disappear, but they will be grist for the mill of your deliverance from the rest of your concepts and conditioning, as discussed in chapter 5 where I said that your understanding of who you are is deepened every time one of these so-called troubles is observed by the Witness so that inner Satsang ensues.

❦

chapter 14

⭑⭒⭑

Myth: Enlightenment Is an Absolute Norm When Describing an Awakened Person

Throughout history, authors of spiritual books have attempted to give an absolute, fixed definition about what happens to a holy man. They didn't have too many to write about, so analyzing this subject was sort of like discussing how many angels could dance on the head of a pin. The Catholic Church came up with volumes of books about what constitutes a saint: They had to have supernatural, miraculous powers while still alive, such as bilocating, levitating, walking through walls, or healing the sick at a distance—you know, just the average. What really clinched sainthood was having the stigmata, where you bled from the same wounds that Jesus did on the cross, or surviving for 40 years on only a daily communion wafer.

However, in analyzing the lives of these saints, I've realized that they were not very happy campers—having special powers didn't add one iota to their personal satisfaction or fulfillment in life. They still felt separated from God and felt like unworthy sinners who had received divine favors. So let's just say the Church accumulated a ton of impractical concepts to use in pondering the Shift.

The Buddhist religion, on the other hand, focused their descriptions of enlightenment on the Buddha's own experience of it as "emptiness." This was a very valid experience for him, and one I wouldn't dare challenge. Where we go amiss is in setting the expectation that no one is enlightened unless they can also soak up the depths of emptiness.

After Ramana Marharshi came along, the Advaita Vedanta folks were looking for the very opposite absolute of the Buddhists. Their description of enlightenment was the "fullness." Again, this is nothing out of line with my own personal experience of the Shift. I would have to agree that it sure does feel like fullness most of the time, but there are also many moments of being aware of the emptiness that somehow creates the fullness.

Now even the transpersonal psychologists are attempting to analyze enlightenment by transcending through the mind rather than through Spirit.

This whole spiritual circus and their related mystery schools seem to imitate the classic story of the six blind men who were touching different parts of an elephant, and while their various descriptions were contradictory, they were each accurate for one part of the elephant.

I love Gurdjieff's attempt at an absolute norm for enlightenment. He says that there are basically three kinds of people in the world: lunatics, vagabonds (also called tramps or the homeless), and householders. Enlightenment is only possible for this latter category, he claims. As a prerequisite to self-realization, you have to handle the third-dimensional life adequately and get out of just living in survival mode. This is what the householders have done. They are the solid citizens of the world. This may sound really weird when you look at the background of most awakened ones in the past, but amazingly enough in my own travels around the world where seekers and finders are coming together in Satsang intensives, only the householders are showing up. Not only are they householders, they are your basic New Age, intense seekers who share a very common story line including gurus; spiritual disciplines; trips to India (with resultant dysentery); and great sensitivity to their diets, bodies, and the ecology in general. Since these are the only ones I've yet dealt with, I might be tempted to describe the prerequisites for Shifting along these lines.

But in my own Shift, I can see clearly that any attempt to classify this experience into an absolute norm that fits everyone is just as futile as to try and catch the wind. It is the limited mind that tries so desperately to understand the infinite vastness of the Shift and reduce it into a format that can comfortably be related to. If I were to put down on paper what qualities I believe are the sine qua non of awakening during this Shift, the spiritual authors of the next millennium would be calling them: *Nadeen's Myths of Enlightenment During the Great Shift of the 21st Century.*

Reality: There Is No Absolute Definition of Enlightenment

There are only relative descriptions. Back to the basics on this one.

Source in the world of appearance has set up the game plan so that every single time it shows up in a limited mind/body organism, it will have a totally unique and one-of-a-kind experience, different from all other previous and future appearances. This being so, it then set up a slight variation in the normal routine around the millennium. In this change of pace, maybe one percent of the population will come into this third dimension with the unique predisposition of a seeker with an intense longing to remember who they are.

This one percent is gradually Shifted into a fourth-dimensional awareness that changes their perceptions but not their predispositions. Why would we ever imagine that these seekers are "cloned" into awakened ones? You know how Source loves diversity.

We don't know the "why" of this Shift. We only know that it is definitely unfolding right now. There is some sort of a unified force field of new energy present now that is affecting millions and millions of seekers and causing them to somewhat simultaneously wake up and remember that *Consciousness is all there is, and I am That.*

And that is the one and only common denominator we have so far, which in no way is an absolute norm of enlightenment. Everything else that describes finders is relative to their unique predispositions and conditioning.

We have to remember we are dealing with Infinite Intelligence here amusing itself over and over again in every new Shifted awareness and in such a way as to be a brand new experience each and every time it happens that it moves from separation to oneness. Forget about putting this experience in a neat little box with a label on it for future generations to use as a model. This Shift is an experience of the Vastness while still contained in a limited mind and body. It contains all opposites, which somehow manage to merge in the middle. There is not one absolute norm you can use to measure a person who claims to be swept away in the Shift. But you might figure out that something is up by the silly little grins for no reason at all that I see at every Satsang!

chapter 15

Myth: When I Am
Enlightened, I Can Manifest
Reality with My Mind

O h God, how we would like this one to be true! Of course it just goes back once again to the original enlightenment myth. First of all, why would this possibility be so attractive to all seekers? Because for our entire lives, our minds have directed us to choose a better way of life and impelled us to do and fix to make this happen. Of course it never got good enough.

Meanwhile, we hear scattered rumors about the mind's power to create your own reality. Now, finally, our mind has something to hope for. If my thoughts create my attitudes, and my attitudes attract my good karma, than all I have to do is control and shape my thoughts so that they are only positive and hold clear intent of what I really want.

And so begins the Herculean task of mantras, affirmations, visualizations, subliminal messages played into your pillow as you sleep, and a host of other fads to shape up your attitude into positive clear thoughts.

Actually, this power of manifesting by affirmations and visualizations works well much of the time. There is, however, this little law of the universe stating that to the exact degree of your expectation, you will experience the inverse proportion in disappointment. There you have it—a nice summary of the third-dimensional attempt to create a perfect reality by the power of your thoughts.

Your mind wouldn't recognize a "perfect" reality if it was living in one. Its only function is to take every thought and divide it into "upside" and "downside," and then try to fix the downside by "doing" something about it. Even if you were the first human being in the history of all the universes ever created to be able to totally direct creation as you saw fit, if your mind functioned as a normal 3D mind, you still would never be satisfied with the reality that you manifested.

Surely this has to be a natural yearning, then, for the seekers to want the grand prize of this enlightenment game. That would give them in the fourth dimension a new power to manifest all their wishes and thoughts, since this is never available 100 percent of the time in the third dimension.

Reality: The True Nature of Acceptance

You are really going to like this reality of 4D manifesting far more than you ever dreamed.

Yes, there is a power to manifest reality in the Shift. In fact, it is in the natural order of the universe as it unfolds your destiny. When you were living life in the third dimension, you were like a fish that lived in a very strong and powerful current (the mind).

Something instinctively made you swim against this current in fear that it might sweep you away if you weren't vigilant enough. And so you swam till were exhausted, fighting to stay abreast of the current and never quite enjoying the scenery because you were basically stuck there in total *resistance* to the ocean's never-ending flow. The mind-set that you inherited told you it is always better to resist the current than to ever just relax into it.

However, your longing to find your true home in the ocean made you swim even harder against the current than 99 percent of the other fish. This intense effort to find your way home resulted one day in a state of such total exhaustion and despair (dark night of the soul) that you gave up trying to resist the current for the first time in your life.

Lo and behold, a miracle ensued. As soon as you quit doing and just relaxed, the current swept you along effortlessly in the most marvelous fashion. It delivered everything you always had to work so hard to get for yourself. It swept you past incredible underwater islands of such beauty that you were amazed because you had no idea of their existence before. You got to meet the most wonderful, exciting other fish who were just as surrendered to this magic current as you, who were also being swept away. And then you realized that at any moment in your life, all of this had been possible and all you'd had to do was *nothing,* just *relax and surrender* to this life-sustaining current.

When you were in control, the most you accomplished was bare survival, and there never seemed to be enough even of that. But when you trusted the current to take care of you, there was abundance at every level.

Let's get out of the ocean for a minute here and discuss this *abundance* phenomenon of the Shift. One of its laws is *synchronicity.* Maybe it was always there before the Shift, and we just didn't notice it. But now I am very aware of its presence and watch it at work continuously, instead of trying myself to manifest abundance.

Here's how it works: When you were like that little fish, you spent all your life resisting what is. I should know; it's a perfect description of me before the Shift. All your energy went into judging, fixing, doing, and resisting what is. There was no real creative energy left over for any playful creations or manifestations. Then the ripe mango fell off the tree and you were Shifted. Now instead of spending all your life-force energy in resistance, you accept what is, just as is, in daily life. All of a sudden, when you are not so busy attempting to direct and control life's unfolding, you have infinitely more energy available to enjoy wherever life takes you. And this life force or current is your own infinite wisdom, which knows exactly what to do for the perfect unfoldment of your destiny.

Back to abundance. I constantly stare in amazement at the perfect synchronicity of events in my life. When I am not beating the bushes in an attempt to find something, it always shows up in the most unexpected way. These are solutions I never could have imagined. Do I actually have more money in the bank now than before the Shift? No, but it sure feels like it. And this feeling of total abundance, without my having to consciously manifest any detail of it, is always present. I just relax into what is, just as is; abundance and the law of synchronicity naturally take care of the rest.

Which dimensional approach to manifesting seems more powerful and natural to you?

❦

chapter 16

Myth: Loss of Personal Identity

A universal concept that has been perpetuated through the ages centers around the loss of mind and personal identity in any self-realization transformation. After all, the whole cause of separation in the first place is the activity of the mind judging, doing, and separating everything within its sensory force field into "others" and "me." The mind is also the cause of all suffering, which can only result when the mind makes a judgment that something is not as it "should" be and offers resistance to what is.

Wouldn't it make sense, then, that on everyone's wish list, the mind part of us would vanish and be replaced by cosmic consciousness that no longer functions through this icky little mind, or at least transcends it?

It makes sense; in fact, it creates expectation, and delivers disappointment if you hold on to it as a concept!

What really happens in the Shift is that the Witness appears—it was always there, just waiting far beneath conscious awareness. Source used infinite intelligence and loving creative energy to develop this mind to work exactly as designed. It does not and will not destroy or stop any of the mind's normal functions, including judgments or a hangover sense of self-identity.

What it does do in the Shift is gradually and subtly move the identity of our awareness from that of the chatterbox little mind who has dominated every aspect of our whole life up to this point, to that of the Witness who peacefully observes all that the mind and 3D reality may present in choiceless awareness.

There is an absolute Knowingness of who you are, and your identity is here in the middle of the mind's limited input and output. But while your sense of Presence may not be totally free, it can still exist freely in the middle of thoughts, judgments, and limited self-identity. If someone calls your name, you still respond. If they ask you your opinion of the latest movie, you might give it two thumbs up. You look in the mirror and you recognize that little inner tube growing around your midriff as *yours*.

Somebody is always home to steer the ship! You are not a walk-in who can no longer identify with this old self or body anymore.

And this is as it should be. Source is here in the third dimension to have a fully limited experience of itself, including the shadow side and all the normal human emotions and instincts. If your mother or your dog dies, you will weep. If you are hungry, you'll eat. If you lose your mate or all your money, you will probably be depressed, but not for long!

There is a big difference now! If a new crisis hits you—and it surely will—after the Shift, it will no longer have the old power of the mind to drag you down into clinical depression, as before your identity was Shifted to that of the Witness.

chapter 17

Myth: Pet Peeves

A t every intensive there comes a time to share our pet peeves with each other. The reason for this process is that if we are learning the dance of "yes" to the big "no" of daily contractions, then it helps to know just what our pet peeves are that make us instantly say "no," maybe even "Hell, no!" as these contractions present themselves.

Here are just a few to give you an idea of what we share:

- Slow drivers in the fast lane who won't move over.

- Shoppers in the 10-item cash-only checkout lane at the supermarket with 27 items, coupons, and food stamps for payment.

- Phone services with a dozen or so menu buttons for selection that never quite reach a live operator.

What is interesting to observe here is the participants who have been describing their own Shift, and feel that it is now a permanent awareness, but get up and read a longer pet-peeve list than anyone else. The seekers who are not yet familiar with the Shift are somewhat shocked due to their concepts around this aspect of enlightenment. The finders may explain that awareness of their pet peeves almost always causes their list to dry up in time. But it seems to be constantly replaced by a quasi-infinite number of new pet peeves that the mind will surely create from its vast well of old concepts about how life is supposed to be.

This is a big difference to understand. Previously the contraction of "no" when a pet peeve would arise was an unconscious, automatic incident. Now after the Shift, the Witness immediately observes the contraction that's underway: "Ah, anger is present. So what!" Thus the "no" of resistance becomes a "yes" of acceptance to what is, just as it is. In that very motion of relaxing into the contraction of the moment, instead of resisting it or trying to fix it, you have the very heart and greatest miracle of this Shift. It is the key to your deliverance from concepts and conditioning, to the rapture of Knowing who you are while still living in a limited mind and body.

For those who are still surprised that Shifted people can write out a pet-peeve list, I ask whether they consider Jesus to be the greatest avatar of all awakened Masters. Of course, they agree. Then I fire off the top ten from Jesus' pet-peeve list. Here are only a few:

- I really get upset when the moneychangers in the temple are ripping off the poor people.

- I hate it when the devil tempts me on the mountaintop and I have to threaten to throw him off.

- It really depresses me when my closest disciples abandon me when I need them most in the garden of Gethsemene.

- That goes double for my Father abandoning me while I hung there dying on the cross.

chapter 18

Myth: Sex After the Shift

Well, surely our sex life must be affected by this Shift. You probably thought it would be replaced by celestial concerts of angel harps and flutes, or at least something of a higher frequency than sex. Another concept bites the dust!

I found the very opposite to be true in my own case, and this is not unique. Before the Shift, sex was just another way to try and fill the bottomless pit of loneliness that the illusion of separation was creating. I needed strong medicine for this, and sex was just one of the many stopgap measures I tried.

True to form, it was also full of the expectation to get something fulfilling out of it, which in turn would always create the disappointment of a peak experience. It got so low on my totem pole of priorities that I had almost lost interest in it by the time I was 53.

Then came my Shift! New energy of a different dimension began coursing through my body. Before this I had used up all available energy in resisting life—suddenly this energy was available for total abundance, for enjoying life just as it is.

The last thing I need now is something like sex to fulfill me. My joy and freedom in life springs from my Knowingness of who I am. That frequency of energy sweeps me away every hour of every day in the peaceful delight of just observing life without having to direct it anymore.

Strangely enough, all this incredible extra energy flowing through me in total abundance must have reactivated my tired old sex drive. But now sex isn't something I need or crave in order to cope with life. Sex is just one of the many ways that my joie de vivre can overflow with my partner in celebrating life. And if she isn't in the mood exactly when I am, then I say to myself, "Poor baby, so be it!" No sense of loss or frustration. If she is, then it becomes a mutual dance of "yes" to life as is.

When I look around, I find so much sexual repression in the tired old conventional wisdom around enlightenment. And do you know what else I find? There are these old-line gurus who preach celibacy as a means of preparing for some eventual and uncertain self-realization, since that is what their whole lineage of gurus handed down along with their spiritual tradition. And sooner or later, a lot of them crash and burn. Even sadder, it's often sex that causes the crash, after their awakening and many years of teaching, often with young female devotees who hold the master on a pedestal of specialness.

But does this then mean that they weren't really enlightened after all? Not necessarily so! You see, we are dealing here with Mother Nature herself, rather than an enlightenment issue. You can't fool Mother Nature! When you try to repress your sexual energy in a foolish attempt to get from here to there, Mother Nature always steps in, and the repressed sex comes back—with a vengeance—enlightened or not.

What may happen now to this poor old guru—who might be scorned or even tossed out of his own ashram, as a result of violating his own commandments—is his Witness within observing this chaos will say: "Ah so! Sex has exploded here, and I got caught with my hand in the cookie jar. Looks like I'm out of here and so what! So be it!"

The Witness is always present, watching in playful amusement at the continual Lila (divine comedy) and chaos of the third dimension. No one ever escapes some chaos in life—but it always comes in perfect balance with some freedom.

chapter 19

~ege~

Myth: Unrecognized As a Saint

This may come as a real shock to all who still haven't realized their promised 15 minutes of fame yet, but after you have Shifted and enjoy absolute, total self-realization as a permanent experience that affects every detail of your life—in other words, the ultimate fantasy of every seeker—your wife and kids may not even notice.

In our inherited need to be "special," we think that surely people will be lining up around the block to touch our foot once we are enlightened, and here is Nadeen saying that maybe no one will even notice. Wait, it gets worse! *You* may not even notice until it is a done deal if you don't know the full reality of this Shift and are stuck in hundreds of old concepts about enlightenment.

It's such a subtle and gradual movement of grace that slowly leads you out of the valley of darkness and into the light of

Knowingness. You don't get an e-mail from God confirming that on February 13, 2002, you will be on the far side of the Shift. Over and over again, thousands of finders at my intensives testify that it took two to four years after the dark night of the soul started to begin to realize that their own Shift was complete and permanent. They did not come to this conclusion in the heat of bliss. It was more like: "Golly, my Witness has been present with me now during every contraction for the last six months. This awareness is even invading my dreams now. In fact, this is finally feeling like *home* all the time now."

The biggest realization of just how far into this Shift seekers may be comes during the intensives when we explore all the concepts and peel the onion layers of conditioning around this theme. They may have even had a lightning bolt of resonance with every word in *From Onions to Pearls* when they read it. But it is usually during a weekend or week-long Satsang that it finally dawns on them: "Wow, here I am in the middle of the Shift, and all along I was afraid it was a middle-age crisis instead!"

Okay, so the wife and kids don't suddenly want to call you "Master" now that you are Shifted. Just remember that whatever predispositions and conditioning that are unique to your makeup before the Shift will still be there after the Shift as well. If you get up grouchy in the mornings before, guess how you will wake up later. Subtle and gradual! This is why no one ever becomes a prophet in their own household. What does change dramatically, though, is your perception of the soap opera we live in, called *Live from the Third Dimension*. But this is an awareness of your own inner wisdom as well as what I call the Presence. This Witness doesn't change anything out there in the real world of illusion, but simply observes it and uses the following three phrases (at least these are the ones my Witness uses) to comment on the following three situations:

1. An act of God is unfolding that involves no human interaction directed at you—maybe you are getting wet in a rainstorm. The Witness says: "So be it!"

2. In the middle of a contraction that does involve another person, the Witness comments: "So what!"

3. Each of the countless times a day that the mind or some other person asks "why" about any and every situation that arises (just as a good little mind is supposed to do), the Witness always responds: "Don't know, don't care!"

That's it. That's the slow and gradual transformation of the Shift. So subtle that you may never get the "proper respect" from your own family or co-workers that your mind says you deserve. So what!

chapter 20

~~~

Myth: The Longing for God

Before the Shift, I used to envision saints and other awakened ones burning up with the intensity of their love for God or the Divine Mother. I was so full of such stories of overwhelming devotion, told through the ages, that I imagined any true saint was probably too dysfunctional to actually carry on with the normal business of raising a family or running a career.

There has always been a lot of emphasis put on this phenomenon of the longing for God before and after enlightenment. I don't want to discount as a myth the intensity of the longing when it is present before the Shift. It is this very longing that has turned us into seekers, and it is only this longing that will instinctively bring us home. Actually, the way this Shift is now occurring, the longing is all you need to return home. There is even a certain New Age movement out there that practices trying to intensify this longing even more in a futile attempt to make "it" happen sooner.

You know about the "doer" routine, trying to fix or make happen anything connected to the Vastness through the resources of this limited mind. Not even the longing for God can be manipulated by humans, whether the goal is to increase it or shut it down completely. Your destiny determines if and when. Period!

The myth we are dissolving here is not about the intensity of the longing *before* the Shift, which certainly does increase. This exposé is about what happens *after* the Shift.

Reality: Home Is Within You

I have been tracking this Shift for a little over six years now and gathering enough new data about the myth of enlightenment to rewrite and turn upside down everything about it we have inherited from the past in both written and oral tradition. What happens to the intensity of our longing for God may be the biggest surprise with respect to this whole fairy tale around enlightenment.

There is a halfway point to this Shift from the third to the fourth dimension. I have drawn an arbitrary line in the sand, and I say once you cross this line you are at least halfway home now. You cross that line the day you realize that after a lifetime of wanting to know the thoughts of God more than a drowning man wants air, you could suddenly care less if you ever wake up or get enlightened.

This realization, unlike the gradualness of the overall Shift, is very sudden and definite. In fact it happens all the time during weekend Satsang intensives. There is a pattern to it we can lay out here.

After years of yearning, searching, doing all the self-improvement seminars, and reading thousands of books, the seeker enters the dark night of the soul in a catatonic state of despair and hopelessness. Now we are forced to just be quiet and listen to the very faint whispers of the Witness, who begins to retrieve the ancient memory of who we are, buried deep in our unconscious but all-knowing intuition.

One of the very first messages that the Witness delivers after we begin to remember that Consciousness is all there is, and *I am That,* is the sequel realization that I am not the "doer" that I always thought I was. Then, almost immediately, from deep within our innate and infinite Wisdom comes the freedom from this search for God. We have found Him! *We* are the God we have always been looking for!

That realization is in itself enough to instantly and forever cut off the longing to go home. We just didn't know until now that we already *were* home. This realization is quite stunning and one that the seekers-turned-finders can always remember afterward, unlike the time and day of their permanent Shift.

It is as if the cosmic pipeline of intense desire just had the valve turned off. The ramifications of *I am That* can now begin to sort out your daily life in this period that I call the deliverance. You have just had your wake-up call, and you are halfway home!

Why do I call this instant turn-off of all longing for God the halfway point? It's now a done deal that the seekers have found within themselves that which they had always looked for without. Yet they are still full of concepts and conditioning about what all this means to the everyday details of living with one foot in the third and the other in the fourth.

It is still going to average another couple of years or more of bobbing in and out of the fourth dimension. The deliverance is going to peel away those onion layers of conditioning until we have a clear, clean, and deep understanding about how Source lives in this limited body of ours as a Witness in choiceless awareness, rather than as a "doer" who manipulates, fixes, and resists life as it presents itself.

The good news from the feedback of these thousands of find-ers I dialogue with in Satsang can assure you that the intensity of the longing that brought you every step of the way through incredible spiritual disciplines and yearning is gone forever the day you remember who you are.

This may sound strange to you right now, but once the long-ing for God is gone, so is all devotion to God. God is no longer out there! Now the Presence within is all that matters. Who are you going to pray to and for what? All is available to you as the Source of all that is, and in such abundance that any prayer that says "Gimme this or that," or "Fix it, please," is ridiculous from my own experience of Presence.

I know that even Maharaj Nisargadatta and Papaji, who were famous as awakened teachers and contemporaries until just recently, did their *pujas* (daily worship) even after they had awakened. But remember, these guys were raised in a culture steeped in such practices and they went along with it afterward because the blades of the fan were still spinning even after the plug was pulled. But me, an American, I don't get it! What is the point of it, anyway?

Because I feel totally free in the absolute Knowingness of who I am, it just doesn't occur to me to do any further kind of spiritual devotion or practices. I have already been there and done my share of that on my way home. But now I am home!

Even if I am sitting quietly in some alone time and it appears that I'm meditating, it's not because of devotion. It's for fun! I just thoroughly enjoy purring alone and quietly, feeling the rich-ness and fullness of Presence. I might want to stop at a famous temple or in a cathedral to check out the architecture, or feel the vibes if the local culture is worshiping. But personal devotion has nothing to do with it. I know where God resides now, and I carry that temple with me like a little turtle—all self-enclosed.

Another important point here: Just because all longing for God dries up for good and you understand at a deep level that

God no longer needs you as Its little helper, doesn't mean that compassion for the sufferings of others also goes out the window with it. On the contrary, for the first and only time in your life, real compassion is now available.

When the seeker lived in separation, what might arise in the face of apparent suffering was really only pity. After the Shift, the understanding and application of *I am That* applies to Consciousness in all its forms. That includes all the other mirrors of yourself out there in 3D land. If I see someone suffering, that is also an aspect of myself I am watching.

The big difference between pity and compassion now is that I can only see the perfection of everything exactly as it is. If Source wants to use this mind/body organism as an instrument of "devotion" to help someone, then Source asks me plain and simple: "Help me!" I am never hesitant or confused about whether it's me that Source is pointing at.

Let me explain to you the two guidelines that have developed in my new dance through life now with a foot in each dimension:

- I ask for nothing.
- I refuse nothing.

If I am supposed to have something, it shows up without my asking for it and always at the perfect time. I call this phenomenon *the law of synchronicity and abundance.*

Then there's the flip side of the coin. If there is something within my resources to give, I cannot refuse a request.

I know this is Source Itself saying: "Help!" The director of our Satsang tour has removed me from all decision-making about our schedule, because I just can't say no to any reasonable request for a Satsang intensive anywhere in the world.

I was recently stretched to the far limits of this guideline when I did two weeks of Satsang in Manhattan. There I was moving around the city by bus and subway, passing dozens of panhandlers on every block while walking to and from various destinations. Chase Manhattan Bank, let alone me, doesn't have enough money to give to everyone begging for a handout. So it boiled down to this: If they looked me in the eyes and asked me in particular for help: "Buddy, can you spare a buck?" I would respond accordingly. But most of them were just holding out a cup and staring vacantly into space. That got me around the block without having to stake out my own corner for replenishment.

I don't know for sure what the last century's "God is dead" philosophical movement was all about. But I do know that all longing for God or even looking for God is definitely dead once you wake up on the other side of the Shift. And it feels like bathing in an ocean of relief and regaining your original innocence. There is no God but Presence!

chapter 21

~e⁹~

Myth: It's Too Simple and Easy to Be True!

We have now arrived at the mother of all myths. I tangle with this during every Satsang and intensive I have ever facilitated. To many of the participants—who have not yet fully experienced the fullness of their Shift, still buried in concepts about enlightenment and struggling with their own dark night of the soul—this whole idea of a Shift appears just too simple and easy to be true. It has got to be more complicated and difficult than what they might be hearing from those of us already past the halfway point of the Shift.

The intuitive part of them resonates with every word that has been shared all weekend. These are not new words, even though they have never heard them spoken before. They resonate at a deep cellular level that I call *ancient memory*. All of their instincts are keenly alive. Their inner wisdom is buzzing with tingles of excitement. They stand on the threshold of crossing over that gap of separation from seeker to the other side where finders soak up the intoxicating energy of Oneness.

Yes, but . . . one last resistance from the mind! Here they are tottering on the brink, nodding their heads in total agreement all weekend long. We are down to the last 15 minutes of closing session. In a final death rattle of the mind's lifelong dominance, when it sees that all identity is being absorbed by the Witness, the mind screams out in defiance: "Wait a minute, here! This is too simple and easy to be true!"

Seekers still in the dark night of the soul seem to have a similar mind-set when it comes to the Shift actually happening to them:

1. *They are "other" oriented.* The Shift can only happen to others, perhaps for the few chosen ones of God. It couldn't be happening to me!

2. *They are "future" oriented.* If a Shift is going to happen to them, it will be down the road. It can't be happening now!

3. *They are "doing" oriented.* Something has got to be wrong with a Shift where you can't make it happen sooner by intentional effort through spiritual disciplines.

   "I've been doing yoga and meditation my whole life trying to make this happen, and now I hear there's nothing to do, just be, understanding is all, and the ripe mango falls off the tree only when it is ready. This ain't right somehow!"

4. *They are "tradition" oriented.* "There's something wrong with a Shift that I can't go down to my local bookstore and read a hundred volumes or so describing

5,000 years of do's and don'ts about something as significant as my own enlightenment."

Actually there are a lot of books about enlightenment. But every book ever written before this Shift
started is full of pure fantasy concepts, purposeful disinformation put out there by Source to keep the seekers
treading water until the time was ripe for this Shift.
Now is that time and all seekers are being Shifted into
4D awareness without effort or disciplines, not *because
of* their tradition or practices, but in spite of them.

5. *They are "image" oriented.* This may sound weird, but
seekers have an image in their mind of what they would
look like as a "saint" and what a "saint" would look like
to them if they met one talking to them about a Shift.
None of them fit their own image of what they would
look like as a saint. I hardly qualify as the "image" either.
Instead of sporting long hair, a beard, and a flowing
white robe, like Jesus and some real "teachers" out there
right now capitalizing on this image, I am bald, wear
warm-up suits, and just got out of prison for making and
selling a drug called Ecstasy. Not very strong credentials
for the "image." But wait, it gets even funnier. . . .

6. *They are "lineage" oriented.* I kid you not. There are
both seekers and so-called teachers out there who question your lineage as a teacher before they can relax into
your message. "Who was your guru, and who was his
guru, etc., etc.?" Now your guru had better be famous
and have lots of "sitas" (which are supernatural powers). It adds to the image if he passed them on to you.
But I have to admit I got Shifted without any guru—in
a federal penitentiary in L.A., smack dab in the middle
of the two most notorious gangs in the world, the Crips

and the Bloods, fighting it out every day. Worse yet, I
didn't have a clue about this whole Shift until it was all
over. The only miraculous power I can describe in
Satsang is my new power to dance "yes" to the "no" of
daily contractions and still maintain a deep, peaceful
freedom from all the judging and doing that my mind
still presents as options.

It is here, in the death rattle of the mind, where the real magic
of Satsang takes over. The mind of the seeker has been struggling
furiously to try and understand just what constitutes the Vastness
of this Shift. But the Knowingness of the Witness comes forward
during Satsang and soothes the frantic effort of the limited mind
to understand a new dimension of awareness. All the objections
raised so far in the intensive begin to settle down into a gentle
understanding that is way beyond the concepts of the mind to
comprehend.

The Witness emerges in the Shift, and the Witness is who you
are. The mind was created to provide the contrast of all human
emotions and has served its purpose well. But this is the point
where the identity of who you really are gets automatically
moved from that of the mind to that of the Witness.

All these crazy concepts surrounding the Shift don't get
explained logically to the mind. Satsang just makes them fade
away into a "don't know, don't care" attitude.

The nicest compliment I regularly receive from seekers
Shifted into finders at the end of an intensive is, "Thank you for
being so ordinary." Now that statement may sound more like a
backhanded compliment, but it truly wipes out the biggest myth
of the whole human predicament.

"Special" is out! "Ordinary" is in! It would never occur to
you to thank someone for being so ordinary until your own
Witness has bathed you in the original innocence, the life-

restoring water of just feeling ordinary for the first time in your life.

End of the myth. The beginning of a reality of now living full time in the fourth dimension.

chapter 22

Just As It Is

As I write this chapter, I sit atop our Costa Rican mountain retreat center. We have just finished a beautiful seven-day Satsang intensive, and the last participant leaves today. The title of this chapter was the main theme throughout the whole week. Our so-called spiritual lives have been completely demystified and rendered utterly simple by the energy field of the Shift. The whole group seemed to really get it, and we went through a lot of Kleenex as each explained how the ramifications of the Shift were now affecting their lives. What could possibly be more simple than this:

- Instead of looking all over the place for God, we know that we are Source in appearance.

- Instead of identifying with the frequency of the mind that judges every situation, we now get to identify with the Presence of the Witness, who observes in choiceless awareness.

- Instead of trying to change every situation into some-thing better and resisting what the mind doesn't agree with, we simply relax into a non-doing attitude and watch in amazement as Life just happens perfectly, all by Itself, without needing our help. Imagine that!

- The key to real happiness in life and the end of all spiri-tual seeking is contained in this phrase: *Embrace life just as it is.*

Sounds pretty simple, doesn't it? Even from a purely intel-lectual understanding, it makes sense if you are swept up in the white waters of the Shift.

Over the last two years, I have seen several thousand heads all nodding in total agreement with smiles of relief and surrender on their faces when I explain this basic message.

But wait a minute! It may be very simple to understand. Is it actually that easy to live out the new dance of "yes" to life's daily contractions and freedoms? This proved to be an interesting week, observing the many varieties of engaging life "just as it is."

One of the participants here had already been part of several weekend intensives over the last two years. He is definitely feel-ing the full impact of the Shift, his life has mellowed out consid-erably as a result, and he merely comes to Satsang for the pure joy of it. However, while down here in Costa Rica, I was able to observe him more closely under all circumstances as we spent about 16 hours a day hanging out as a group. What I actually saw under these conditions was astounding. Although he seemed to be flowing with Life in the "major, important" events, he acted like a total control freak in life's "mini" happenings at least 50 times a day.

What this means is that every time there was an opportunity for a preference, the mind demanded and acted out that preference in a controlled and "doer"-like fashion. In the dining hall, it was "Please lower the music!" or "You are sitting in my spot," or "I want to go first for massage," and this guy was constantly late for every single event. Somehow an attitude of passive/aggressive manipulation seemed to permeate this person getting whatever he wanted in every situation that presented itself.

Now why wasn't I surprised when this person complained one night at Satsang that he was bored and kept falling asleep. Even though this had never happened to me before, it made perfect sense now. Another factor is also pertinent here: Although a fit and flexible athlete, his back just suddenly went out in a debilitating way just before his Shift began. What's the connection?

As it happens, I am currently involved in presenting workshops jointly with Dr. John Veltheim, an Australian who developed the "BodyTalk" process for healing any and all ailments known to the human body, in a seemingly miraculous manner.

The reason I am so enthusiastic about his methodology is that he is using the very same inner wisdom of Source-in-appearance to heal the physical and emotional body that I am using to heal the apparent separation between man's mind and the Oneness.

Now here is the amazing part, and the connection I refer to. He proves that with each patient there is almost always a link between the particular ailment and a major contraction of resistance still locked into bodily memory. Once the BodyTalk process releases that trauma of resistance to whatever happened, then the healing becomes virtually spontaneous and permanent.

I can well imagine my friend's back going south when he was headed north because of his tremendous resistance to Life just as it is; I can still observe in him in all the small stuff, and as we know life is mostly small stuff. Now this could well be the pot calling the kettle black, as I see myself as also being the epitome of "anti-Life just as it is" before my own Shift was complete.

The whole point here that struck me so clearly is this:

> Even if you think you get "it";
> even though you know for sure you are being
> swept away by the force of the Shift;
> even if it seems like you can now embrace life's
>   tragedies;
> it is really in the dance of *yes* to the hundred or
>   so small daily contractions through which
>   your deliverance is actually proceeding.

You may amaze yourself when you dance "yes" to the contraction of losing your job, and then argue with the waitress at Denny's to seat you in the roped-off section. You just managed to dance a jig of "yes" as your mate left you in the lurch, and then bristled with indignation and a vocal complaint when that little old lady tried to get through the express line with double the allowed number of items. You get the picture!

Shifting from the third dimension to the fourth means that once you realize and remember who you really are—Source in appearance—then it doesn't really matter what you are doing or not doing. You are temporarily limited to a certain mind/body organism with a unique set of DNA and predispositions, and that's how it is. You watch life unfold in front of you moment by moment. Instead of controlling and manipulating the hundreds of possible preferences you have in any day of the week, you simply allow life to happen—just as it is!

I can assure you that trying to control life is a surefire way to suffer—and that includes suffering boredom. Embracing life just as it is results in the only recipe for true and lasting happiness that I know of.

Now, if we are going to talk about the secret formula that positively assures happiness on Earth, I can see many hands waving in the air. Now we are touching on everyone's main driving force and fantasy. You might want this formula to include a loving relationship with your soulmate, good health, reasonable intelligence, the finer things in life that financial abundance can provide, and everything else we think we want. Not a chance! I harbored all these fantasies and more before my Shift, and they never delivered for more than ten minutes at a time.

What I found out regarding a true, real, and permanent experience of happiness lies in a miracle of grace that allows you to embrace life—just as it is, right when it is happening—in spite of the mind's preferences!

I never ever felt any loving gratitude for any of the happenings in my life before the Shift. Now, every day I feel deep, loving gratitude that is not connected to any condition or event. Why so? The Presence of my Witness is the power that can now make this possible as life unfolds, just as it is.

Quite surely, my friend in the intensive would never consider himself a control freak. He probably feels that he is dancing just as fast as he can to life, and that's probably a fact. It just doesn't occur to him yet that he still spends the greater part of every day resisting life's teeny little contractions when it doesn't meet his preferences. Of course he can see the big events as a crisis to embrace. He just doesn't get it yet that also embracing the mini-contractions is an integral part of his deliverance. When will he get it? When it's time for that ripe mango to fall off the tree all by Itself!

chapter 23

The Laws of Energy That Run This World of Appearance

Source at rest is an impersonal energy that is formless, expanding infinitely, and aware of itself in a state that the ancients describe as bliss. My choice of words might be more like a deep peace—this is what the Presence feels like to me, instead of bliss. At some point Source had a dream of pure mental energy that created another reality that we call the world of appearance. In effect, Source now gets to have a very personal, unique, and one-of-a-kind experience that each human mind/body provides.

However, the infinite Intelligence behind this dream of appearance is still an impersonal energy—hence, the need for certain laws that cause the universe to run on autopilot without the need for some personal entity that we always believed to be

"God," dispensing justice and favors to those that merit them.

In the six years of deliverance since my own Shift began, I have been fascinated by an awareness of at least a dozen of these universal laws at work, without any prior knowledge in all my years of searching for the truth. As I repeat over and over in Satsang: *All wisdom is totally available to those who tune in to the Presence of the Witness in silent Satsang.*

The Law of Balance Between Freedom and Limitation

This is the cornerstone law of energy that keeps the entire world of appearance spinning along nicely in a juicy but balanced way. This law's offspring, the law of contrast, is discussed below.

With no one in particular pulling the puppet strings in the very unique lives of six billion earthlings, and maybe even countless more life forms out there in other galaxies, Source has infused every single atom and molecule in the entire universe with its own Consciousness, infinite Intelligence, and eternal Wisdom. That means that every atom interacts with every other atom in a harmonious and balanced way in line with the original game plan.

Briefly restated, the law of balance regulates a process whereby Source will have a unique, one-of-a-kind experience in every life lived, although each life will equal out to a perfect balance in total positive and negative experiences.

I'm not quite sure why (who cares, anyway!) but this first law about balance is the most difficult one for someone just starting their Shift to understand. They can't comprehend how Attila the Hun and St. Francis of Assisi ended up with the same ratio of freedom to limitation in each of their lives.

Folks tend to believe that they have either a much better or a much worse life than anyone else they know. But with a little deliverance, these concepts fall away as their Witness overrides the judgments of the mind. I remember one intensive participant who started out challenging this law and ended up writing a whole book about the perfection of it all.

Please understand that this law assures the poor limited mind that all is well, even in spite of all the seeming chaos around it at times. The roller coaster of life has equal ups and downs and provides for a rich experience of all the emotions, positive and negative, and an equal balance of freedom and limitation.

Please don't feel sorry for anyone in the entire universe, and please don't envy anyone out there for seeming to have it better than you do. It's just not so! Of course I agree that to the mind it looks as if other lives are better or worse, but the reality is truly balanced. You would have to walk a mile in every man's moccasins to really know what each person is feeling as various events unfold. Your limited mind just can't play out a quasi-infinite number of life's scenarios. Therefore, you can't get verification of this law from your mind. It only comes to me in the deep silence of Satsang with my Witness, who delights in pointing out how perfectly balanced this whole life experience really is.

The Law of Contrast

This is the offspring of the previous law. Maybe they are even twins—who knows! But Source does operate in the world through a definite law of contrast.

Whatever experience you may have as an emotional high or low point, you will also experience the polar opposite of that very same emotion at some point in your life. What is a little different here is that the law of freedom and limitation provides for a total balance of all experiences by the end of your life.

The law of contrast merely states that for every high or low, good or bad, happy or tragic experience your mind may encounter, the contrasting emotion or feeling is waiting for you somewhere down the road. That is why I love to stress that this whole experience of the Shift takes you out of the roller coaster of life's emotions, leaving you cruising in a very neutral space that I call *choiceless awareness.*

Yes, you may encounter what your neighbors would describe as the ecstasy of accomplishment or the agony of defeat. But to someone living in a Shifted perspective, either one of those poles feels pretty neutral. Within the awareness of Presence, you are so deep in the Ocean of Consciousness that events on the surface don't take you out of that place of peace and acceptance of life just as it is.

There will be contractions and flashes of bliss, but now they don't connect to where you really live—at peace in the Presence of Source.

The Law of Humiliation

As you know by now, all these laws are designed to keep life in balance and at the same time provide a very juicy playground for Source in this world of appearance. Most important of all, they run on autopilot all by themselves as conscious, intelligent forces of energy that originate from the impersonal domain of Source.

The game plan is set up as follows: To be born into the human predicament guarantees you a mind, which has its own third-dimensional life even within our essence as pure Satchitananda. This little rascal is born to raise nonstop hell by judging every thought it receives and then trying to do something about the aspect it either likes (desires) or doesn't (resists). This function of comparing everything creates polarity, which in turn creates the illusion of separation.

As the mind begins to spin, a personality is formed early on in life that really believes it has free choice and is the "doer," the captain of its own ship. Naturally this fantasy creates the heart of the whole human predicament where we believe with all our intelligence that we are driving our own vehicle on the freeways of life. All the time, we are really the little kid strapped into the car seat with a toy steering wheel, pretending to drive.

The law of humiliation dovetails with the law of freedom and limitation when our ego starts puffing up like a Macy's Thanksgiving Day parade balloon with self-importance.

This happens when we set goals and think we have achieved or even overachieved them. We then begin to attribute to the power of our mind our good fortune in life and to take full credit for it.

Enter the dragon—a dragon of humiliation that fears no man, whether he be the Pope, the president, or the "holiest" of saints. If you are out of balance in your own evaluation of yourself as someone special, then I absolutely guarantee you that this dragon will be paying you a visit, and probably sooner rather than later.

I need only cite a few examples here that will make the law of humiliation perfectly clear. Does President Bill Clinton come to mind here? He is the leader of the most powerful and rich nation on the planet. He has everything a man can aspire to: ultimate power, a beautiful family, health, wealth, fame, and the esteem of the whole world. Obviously he must have been feeling pretty special about all this stuff. Our dragon, wearing the guise of Monica, pays him a visit, and overnight he is the laughingstock of the whole world. Result: a choked-up penitent begging the world for forgiveness as he surveys the charred ruins of his world. The law of humiliation never fails. Do you think Nixon got a similar visit from the dragon?

There was an interesting statistic that made the headlines in the Clinton scandal, which really impressed me. When the FBI examined the stain on Monica's dress, it was proven to be Clinton's by DNA analysis with an accuracy rate of seven and a half trillion to one. What does that say about our one-of-a-kind uniqueness in the human predicament? He is so unique that in more than a million other planets, each with a similar number of inhabitants, we couldn't find another match-up with the same DNA.

I was involved in my younger days with Shri Bhagwan Rajneesh, also known as Osho, as part of my "gurus are special" phase. I saw a truly awakened master convey a unique and refres0hing message of freedom that a hungry little spiritual community had yearned for. Then, this community grew into a million devotees all proclaiming how "special" Osho was, and showering him with more money and adulation than the law allows. Along with the other *sanyasins* (or those who have taken vows or sanyas in order to self-realize), I would line up along the road every day for miles just to wave and swoon while he drove by in a new and different Rolls Royce. He was guarded by a phalanx of Uzi-toting bodyguards surrounding his Rolls while a helicopter gunship hovered above.

Yet I know absolutely that Osho started off in his awakening and deliverance by enjoying the delicious oasis of feeling just ordinary. But fame and power are like an infectious airborne virus; they permeate and spread. Fifteen thousand devotees standing in a Satsang hall and screaming your praises as the new avatar can turn even a saint's head. Obviously something happened to cause our dragon friend to visit Osho and instantly knock him off his throne. Disguised as the U.S. Feds, it came in, arrested him, hauled him off in chains and shackles, and held him secretly in various prisons without even granting him his lawful rights. Meanwhile, his whole empire crashed down around him and burned as his followers left in droves, bitterly disappointed.

Nothing unusual here. Just our friendly dragon of humiliation keeping everything in perfect balance so that the ego personality doesn't stray too far from its center point.

By now you get the picture. But the law of humiliation doesn't just work on the big picture of life. It also thrives in even the smallest of details in our daily lives. As soon as we begin to think we are "hot stuff," something always happens to open our eyes to the reality of the human predicament. It could be as loud as a heart attack or as quiet as a flat tire on the way to work. But the law of humiliation will get our attention, one way or the other!

Please don't feel that this law of humiliation is the avenging angel of the Lord. Quite the contrary, it is merely the loving, intelligent energy of a finely tuned and perfect universe. It makes sure that every single time Source is in appearance as a human, the experience will not only cover a unique band of emotional experiences, but will never, ever get so out of control that it will adversely affect the harmony of the entire dance. The law of humiliation is our guarantee that we won't ever get too crazy with our own "specialness." After all, we are the Source of it all and that is the only specialness that really matters to our own happiness and fulfillment.

chapter 24

The Law of Karma

At the heart of Eastern spirituality is the focus on *karma*. The Sanskrit word in itself simply means "cause and effect"— nothing to do with spiritual overtones. However, also at the heart of Eastern spirituality are strong undertones of separation, in the form of humanity reaching out to God through spiritual practices.

This means that if good deeds are performed, good things should come to you, not only in this life, but even in future ones. The reverse applies to bad deeds—you might even come back as a three-headed toad in your next life if you screw this one up badly enough.

So why the strong emphasis on karma? Because the mind totally identifies with the results of karma as its own creation, whether good or bad. That's what good little minds are supposed to do!

Naturally, when the New Age message began to surface in the early 1960s, karma became the capstone of its whole philosophy and also its main focus. This hyped the realization that we were not the victims in life that the organized religions seemed to indicate.

We alone are responsible for our thoughts, and our thoughts create our attitudes, and our attitudes create our reality. We are no longer helpless little sheep waiting on divine favor! We can create our own life to the extent that we can control our thoughts and attitudes. Well, good luck! No matter what your intellect may indicate, no one yet born into the human predicament has been able to control their thoughts. Transcendental Meditation and a host of other techniques became popular only because they were sold as a way to control the mind, or at least slow it down somewhat.

At first, you may even have felt hopeful or liberated by this message of personal freedom through mind control. As I said, it is an even bigger hype than what the organized religions were trying to sell. The more you focus on your separation as the "doer" trying to control and manipulate your world, the deeper into suffering and despair you will descend.

That's the law of karma. If you believe that you are responsible for your actions and that your actions deserve either praise and reward or blame and punishment, then you will suffer to the degree that you attempt to control those actions.

That's the bad news about the law of karma!

And now, here's the good news: The end of the law of karma is here and now!

That's right. In the Shift from the third dimension to the fourth, a very significant release happens as soon as you wake up and realize that you are only pure Awareness and Consciousness. You are definitely not the "doer" in the third dimension of all your so-called deeds and their seeming results.

When you no longer identify with yourself as a mind who judges and reacts to every thought with either desire or resistance, a strange and wonderful occurrence happens to our ancient law of karma. It's all over! No more fear of reprisals or hope for a reward. You are free to enjoy and celebrate life without consequence because there is no "ego you" in charge of life anymore. Wake up, know who you really are, and then you can do whatever you like. You are only Source in appearance, and that little chatterbox-monkey of a mind no longer controls your life.

Cause and effect will still be there. That's how the whole human predicament is programmed. An action that we'll call a "cause" occurs and then a "reaction" we can call an effect will result. What is this reaction all about? Each and every one of us is programmed at the factory to be absolutely unique, using both DNA strands and later societal conditioning.

Whenever a "cause" or stimulant engages our mind, we will react automatically by our programming. This is true of our actions even after the Shift. Our reaction buttons may have been sufficiently modified by the higher frequency of the Shift to now react in a new and different way. We may no longer identify with ourselves as the "doer," and thus our reactions may be different. Cause and effect—action and reaction—are always there. But the law of karma isn't because we don't identify any more with mind's judgment regarding the catalyst of action or thoughts. Therefore, reaction is still there, but we are free of the consequences.

The identity is now with the Presence of our Witness. We laugh at the prospect of good or bad karma like a child who eventually learns that there is neither a Santa Claus, nor a boogie man in the dark.

We are free now. The law of karma only affects the third dimension of separation. There is only Oneness now in this Shift—no more karma!

chapter 25

The Law of Desire

The law of desire springs directly from the law of judging. You already know that if you are born into the human predicament, you come fully equipped with a fully functioning mind that was designed by infinite Intelligence for a dual purpose. A good little mind receives every thought, the mental energy of Source Itself, instantly judges it, and then breaks it into a polarity of opposites. This immediately engages a movement toward *doing* something about the pole that it judges as good. I call this function *desire*.

Simultaneously, another movement engages to do something about the other pole, judged as negative; I call that function *resistance*. It would be logical to think that this "doing" mechanism that is a result of judging might be evenly balanced between desire and resistance, but it just isn't.

Have you noticed in your own life that over 80 percent of your available energy goes into resisting what you don't like about life, and only about 20 percent is left over for pursuing what you want? Have you also noticed how your mind almost always prefers to obsessively dwell on the negative aspect of every situation? If so, don't feel like the Lone Ranger; this is how the human predicament usually functions.

As a direct result of your mind automatically judging and desiring or resisting every thought that passes through your little antennae, Source has unlimited access to the soap opera of life's wide range of human emotions and feelings. And this is as it should be. How do I know that? Because life is just as it is!

The definite downside to the law of desire is that you will continue to experience suffering from every situation that the mind judges as unacceptable. There is no way out of suffering as long as the mind is the dominant identity we utilize in the third dimension. That doesn't mean that Source is just a cruel, masochistic, or practical joker by designing a mind that always paints itself into a corner of suffering. The law of contrast, which we talked about previously, is also at work here.

You, as a limited mind/body organism that feels separate, are guaranteed to wake up and remember who you really are. This will happen at the moment of your death when the little bubble who floats on the sea of Consciousness pops and realizes with a big *Ah-ha!* that it is and always was the entire ocean. Or as a seeker with intense longing to know and realize yourself now, it will happen as a result of this new force field I call the Shift. Be aware that while you still have a foot in each dimension, it is more like a string of little "Ah-ha's" instead of just one big one at the passing. These little ones are what I call the *deliverance*.

chapter 26

The Law of Love

B efore we get to talk about love, we have to start by redefin-
ing it away from all the contamination it gets from the third-
dimensional perspective. Simply stated, my only definition of
love is embracing whatever is, just as it is, and only because it
is—without conditions that it be other than what it is. Now that's
love! This doesn't mean your mind has to even like it or feel
attracted by it. Love is a very neutral experience in the ambience
of the fourth dimension.

This is the interesting part of my story, which you have been
waiting for your whole life of longing and seeking. When the first
insights of the Shift start to grab you, you will experience the
subtle transition from the law of judging whatever is, to the
delight of embracing what is—the law of love. Oh, does this ever
feel delicious! What a relief to feel enough Presence as the
Witness to embrace life just as it is, instead of identifying with a
mind that can only judge it as lacking.

You know you have crossed over dimensional borders when you start being aware that your power has Shifted from the mind to the Presence.

Just as the law of judging spawns an offspring called *desire,* so does its counterpart, the law of love, have a wondrous child called the law of inspiration. Just reflect for a moment how you have been tormented your whole life by constant desires that you couldn't fulfill, or even if you did, they never delivered satisfaction for more than ten minutes.

As Buddha said 2,500 years ago: "Desire is the root of all suffering." I see it from a slightly different angle: Resistance is the cause of all suffering, because the ratio of resistance to desire is more like 80:20.

Anyway, just imagine this scenario: in the Shift, all your desires are transformed into a new state of awareness under the law of inspiration. Desires try to compulsively drive you on, while inspiration is the gentle attraction of the heart to its own manifested unfoldment of destiny. Desire involves an attachment to the outcome of the *doing,* and if you don't succeed, it can be as painful as a root canal without anesthesia. Inspiration guides you instinctively to your bliss without fear of failure, because any and all outcomes are still the same to the Witness.

The difference between being driven by desire and guided by inspiration is such a contrast that the mind doesn't even get to ask whether something is really inspiration or just another desire. It is too obvious for doubt to enter.

I am a man of strong addictive/compulsive predispositions. I know what it feels like to be out of control when the mind and its desires are the force behind your life—it sure doesn't feel very comfortable. All the more impact, then, that this story carries. In the Shift, I can assure you, even a lifetime nightmare of being driven by desire can be transformed into a loving dance of acceptance, by simply changing partners from the mind to gentle inspiration.

chapter 27

The High-Five Encounter

For the first four years of deliverance after my Shift, I was
reluctant to share with anyone this process I call the High-
Five encounter. After all, my whole spiritual life as a seeker had
consisted of various practices, all designed to get you from here
to there. But the High-Five perfectly contrasted the seeker
"doing," and the Shift happening all by itself with absolutely no
help from "me." Four more years of prison provided a very quiet
place inside the Presence of the Witness to watch my deliverance
slowly peel away the countless layers of concepts previously
acquired with my active little monkey-mind. And so I was cau-
tious about putting anything out there that even resembled another technique to confuse the seekers.

For one thing, the results of using the High-Five are rather
dramatic. Since we still have one foot in the third dimension, the
mind is quick to surmise that because contractions can be painful,
and this "technique" can dissolve them at their very root, well,

let's use it for instant relief. But High-Five doesn't work if only used by the mind to heal itself.

What can bring us more instantly present than a contraction of the mind caught up in judging a situation and then resisting it? It's our "wake up and don't go back to sleep" call from our Witness as many times a day as the contractions flood the mind.

By using the High-Five encounter, we get to look consciously and with full awareness at every contraction for what it really is, namely an invitation from Presence to examine life in the human predicament with a new perspective of Source. What previously provided 100 percent of life's miseries is really your new passport to the rapture of the fourth dimension, countless times a day.

In case someone out there isn't familiar with what "high five" means in American slang, I'll explain it here. The best example would be two athletes spontaneously celebrating a goal or touchdown. They leap in the air toward each other, while extending their right hand open-palmed. They slap each other's palm, usually with a loud "Yes!"

In our case the encounter takes place in the meeting of a contraction with the Presence of the Witness. They symbolically join in a collaborative "Yes" to life just as it is. There is an exchange of inner wisdom that floods the pilgrim's understanding, and the process of deliverance continues to dissolve the concepts that caused the contraction in the first place.

It doesn't feel like I invented this High-Five encounter in any conventional sense. It just became plain to me that this process naturally occurs whenever the Witness is present during a contraction. After watching it for almost six years now, I've started to share it with participants and they love it.

The feedback has been quite decisive. High-Five is a natural outcome of the Shift now underway. It is natural in the third dimension for the mind to create a contraction out of every concept it holds about how life "should be." It is now also natural for the Witness to use that same contraction to deepen our understanding of the fourth dimension and life just as it is.

To describe the mechanics of the High-Five encounter, I use our five fingers:

Pinkie finger—When the contraction has your mind and emotions strongly in its grip, stop everything for a few minutes. Know that life is designed by Source, but you are dealing with it as dictated by the mind in this moment. The contraction is coming from a concept the mind has about how life should be. If you relax into the contraction, instead of trying to make it go away or resolve the issue that you think is causing it in the physical world, you can start by just feeling the emotion going on in you. Go ahead, really feel it! What does it feel like to be angry or disappointed without squirming out of it?

Now go below the initial feeling brought up by the contraction and see how deep it goes and what is really causing it. If you follow any contraction deep enough you will find that they all lead to the same place: fear! There's not enough love, security, money, or time!

Ring finger—The next step is the dance of "yes" to a very big "no!" that has momentarily commanded the full attention of your mind and feelings. Mind you, I am not saying: "Yes, this feels okay." The Witness is simply acknowledging, "Yes, anger is present, and that's life just as it is."

But before we can even do that much, there is a prelude to the dance of "yes." Whatever is causing this contraction is life as it is, and not necessarily as the mind wanted it. So there has been a real loss here. Life didn't conform to your expectations. Take a moment to grieve for the mind's loss. Feeling another emotion such as grief allows for a full, passionate embrace of the contraction to come through as the new dance of "yes" to the "no."

You are in for a real treat the first time your Witness allows you to relax into something your mind has been fighting your whole life. To feel rage from the mind while knowing that all is well, as the Presence of the Witness overrides the seriousness of the situation with an amusing "yes," is your introduction to the fourth dimension.

Sometimes when a potential sponsor for a weekend intensive calls me to talk about details, they ask what my supernatural powers are, now that I have a foot in the fourth dimension. Of course, this is coming from the myths about enlightenment. I always reply the same way: My greatest (and only) power is the ability to dance "yes!" to the "no!" of life's daily contractions. And this is also my greatest joy.

Middle finger—Now that "yes" is present amidst the contraction, check in with the Witness to see if any special Satsang is also there for your benefit and deliverance. This is the moment of opportunity for the inner Wisdom of your Presence as Satchitananda to bust into space dust that concept that caused the contraction in the first place. When I check to see if any Satsang is present, a new understanding always comes forward about life just as it is. It may be the very same situation that caused the last five days' contraction—yet I get new and different Satsang about it each time I check in.

Index finger—After I digest the Satsang about this situation, I next ask my Presence if there is any "loving gratitude" present alongside this ugly ole contraction. Amazingly enough, there is always so much loving gratitude present that it completely overwhelms whatever downside emotion I may have been feeling. This is where an inner giggle bubbles up as the Witness observes how serious the mind is trying to be about this contraction and how delicious the loving gratitude feels in the middle of that. Basically, this is the point where the contraction usually dissolves with a "poof" right before your mind's eye.

Thumb—As a final farewell to the contraction that so conveniently allowed me to experience life in this moment just as it is—instead of just how my mind wanted it to be—comes a gentle but powerful feeling of Presence as a reminder of who I really am. How does that make my foot that's in the third dimension feel? Like a cat curled up in the sun just purring with contentment. How did I get to feel so good all of a sudden? Because of a High-Five encounter between one of those mysteries of life called a *contraction,* and the Presence of my Witness using this occasion to share Satsang, loving gratitude, and a deep connection to the reality of who I really am.

At first my Witness used this process on almost every contraction that appeared. I watched in awe and amazement as each contraction would go "poof" and then dissolve in the wisdom of Presence. As time went by, the normal little contractions were not critical enough to trigger this mechanism because the only response of my Witness became: "That's life, so what!"

By now the High-Five only kicks in if the contraction is an unusually big one, generally when my first reaction to a stressful situation is one of total overwhelm. But the magic of the High-Five is still there, constantly available for use in examining what could possibly trigger a feeling of overwhelm after spending so much time cruising with a foot in each dimension.

And each time I look at the current contraction as the Witness, the force of that overwhelm dissolves in front of the mind within a few minutes. Certainly there are situations where the impact of the contraction is so great that it lasts for days, especially in the case of grief. Yet even within the natural grieving for a loved one is the ever-sweet Presence of the Witness holding your hand, reassuring you that even this is life just as it is.

Chapter 28

Interview: Shifting Without Effort

Lynn Marie Lumiere and John Wins interviewed Nadeen for their forthcoming book, *The Awakening West,* published by Blue Dove Publishing. The questions they asked give further insight and perspective on all you've just read.

Lynn Marie: At the core of all spiritual searching is the question, "Who am I?" What, if any, answer have you found?

Nadeen: Is this a trick question? I don't even know who I am or where I am anymore. But there is a Shift of consciousness, and it involves simply remembering who we are. Until that happens, nothing else is possible. I call awakening "the Shift" because these words *awakening* and *enlightenment* are so loaded today. Nobody knows what you are talking about when you say them anymore.

The core event of this Shift is the day when, by grace, we wake up and remember that consciousness is all there is. Consciousness is all there is, and *I am That,* and so is everyone else! It sounds so simple. It seems that it couldn't possibly be this simple; after all, we've had 5,000 years of spiritual discipline. But it is that simple. There is a force field present in the world right now that is allowing this ancient memory to come forward. It has always been purposefully, by infinite intelligence, kept in the background.

So the moment you remember who you are, that you are not a third-dimensional, separated being even though that has been your life experience, the Shift takes over. The part that may be sudden is the remembrance. One day you don't remember, and the next day you do; but that is only a baby step in this whole process. It is the very beginning. And each month and year after that, you look back at that first day you started to remember, and it really feels like a baby step. After that remembering, what I call the "deliverance" takes over.

Lynn Marie: You said there is a Shift from the third dimension into a fourth dimension. Could you explain what you mean by that?

Nadeen: First I have to explain what I mean by a third dimension. The third dimension is set up by infinite intelligence to make it seem as if your identity is just the mind—whatever the mind presents. The way it judges; the way it separates into polarities; the way it gives you the illusion of free will, control, and choice; the way it constantly doubts everything from your intuition—that's the third dimension. There is no way to get out of the third dimension by yourself. There is no discipline invented that can get you there. No enlightened master can take you with him. The Shift into the fourth dimension is the change of identity from the dominance of the mind to the presence of the Witness, where you become an observer of life just as it is. Here, you are in choiceless awareness watching the third dimension happen, and the mind is simultaneously making its same judgments, but you no longer identify with them. The presence of a Witness is incredible because it produces a deep knowingness—beyond the mind, beyond experience, beyond explaining like I'm trying to do now—which can see through the mind and is not pulled into it.

This doesn't mean it can't feel contraction. Contractions are just as present after the Shift as before. The difference is that you no longer identify with them—there is a simple witnessing of, "Ah, anger is present, joy is present; that's the mind doing its thing like all good little minds are supposed to do." So you don't identify with it. This is the greatest miracle of the fourth dimension.

Lynn Marie: You are saying that it is a miracle to have this Shift take place. . . .

Nadeen: Yes. There is no way to disidentify from the mind by using human intelligence or intentional effort. The mind cannot get rid of itself. Its function is to stay on top, in control. It takes some sort of supernatural power greater than walking on water, or any other miracle you can think of, to simply watch life happening, and instead of judging and trying to make it better, to simply embrace life just as it is, without trying to fix it. The nature of the mind is to fix and make better. The fourth dimension is simply watching life unfold without the slightest need to fix or make better. And that is the only secret of happiness there is. It is not possible to be happy in the third dimension, no matter what the conditions. If you are not in the space of embracing life as it happens, then you cannot be happy, because all of life is an equal balance of freedom and limitation. Every person, no matter how enlightened or dense they are, has the same balance of freedom and limitation—that part never changes. The miracle is this ability to dance "yes" to the "no" in the middle of disaster. That is the Shift that is the fourth dimension and *it has never happened before.*

Even in the tales of saints and masters, I am not sure how far they got in this, because there was still an agenda of shoulds and shouldn'ts, do's and don'ts; still trying to control life. And if you look at what history has presented us regarding the saints and the masters, they didn't always seem like a very happy lot, did they? The saints still considered themselves sinners not worthy of the great grace of mystical union. Hey, when I woke up, I knew I was totally worthy. Because I knew I was the Source of it all. There was no possibility of being an unworthy sinner or needing to control life any more. So, to the degree that my deliverance has brought me more and more into harmony with embracing every detail of life, that has been my degree of resulting happiness, joy, peace, freedom, or whatever else you want to call it.

Lynn Marie: You say that this Shift to the fourth dimension where there is an ability to say "yes" to the "no" in the middle of a contraction has never happened before. From what I have read and studied, this is not new; it's just becoming more widely known, especially in the West. Teachings that discuss letting everything be as it is, and allowing it to be liberated in that acceptance, have been available for a long time. The Buddhist Dzogchen teachings, for example, discuss this.

Nadeen: If that's in there, then how could the Buddhists have 10,000 rules of do's and don'ts about life? You come to such a place of total freedom in the Shift that there isn't one single do or don't possible because it's all Source in appearance. That means that everything is exactly the way it's supposed to be, everything is happening just as it is. So, to put do and don't in there means you might have a rather limited experience of enlightenment.

John: I think the distinction here is that in Buddhism there are teachings for every stage of development. The Buddha taught for about 40 years, and he taught many people in different stages of development. One thing he taught was right conduct or character so that people could stabilize in that before they could get touch with their yearning and move toward the next stage. That aspect of Buddhism has a lot of do's and don'ts, a lot of ethical dimensions. Then with Dzogchen and Zen, especially Dzogchen, it's not that way. It's a much more direct introduction to the presence of awareness and living from that, letting things be as they are. These teachings are new to the West, however. They have been around for a long time, but have spread to the West only since China's invasion of Tibet.

Nadeen: There is probably nothing that anybody can say that is new under the sun. Let's just put it this way: In the mainstream spirituality that is available to New Agers, I haven't heard it. And for that reason, I quoted verses from the *Tao Te Ching* in my first book. These are 3,000-year-old verses saying exactly what I'm saying. And in [this book] I have put in verses from the *Ashtavakra Gita,* which are just as old and also say exactly the same thing. The problem is that you have to be Shifted to even understand it. If you are not, it doesn't even make sense. So, these truths have been around, but they haven't emphasized the non-doing and accepting of life just as it is. What has been emphasized, however, is the doing, the disciplines, or, even less noteworthy, the states of nirvana, bliss, and *samadhi,* which are really only a minuscule part of it. The sooner they are gone the better; they are peak experiences. What you live with in the Shift is the Presence, which is not a peak experience and never goes away. Anything that distracts you out of that, including bliss-outs, is just a blip. It's not part of the Shift.

Lynn Marie: It's true that what has been emphasized is the doing and the bliss. There is such a wide spectrum of experience available to have as a human being in this life. Being in bliss all the time would limit our range of experience. Bliss is only one small part of the spectrum. What awakening seems to be about is being more fully and totally alive in every sense, fully experiencing the whole spectrum of human experience.

John: In reading *From Onions to Pearls,* we were struck by the paradox of how you found freedom in a situation where your worldly freedom was extremely curtailed. Would you please describe how that came about for you?

Nadeen: I think that what is even more paradoxical, John, is the fact that when I was living on my mountaintop in Costa Rica with basically unlimited money and power, I did not find freedom there. It didn't happen until I found myself confined in an overcrowded hellhole of a prison. Certainly it is a paradox, and Source's favorite dance in this third dimension is through paradox. The way paradox works is that you figure out through human logic how things would work the best, and then do just the opposite. That seems to be the way Source plays. So, in prison every freedom was not always taken away, but my life felt like it was always in jeopardy, because I was in a violent prison, and not by accident. Waking up in those conditions was the greatest validation of freedom I could have imagined. Had I gotten out of prison, gone back to my mountaintop, and then all of a sudden had the experience of awakening, I might have thought, *Well, maybe it is connected with being free from jail.* I was at the beginning of my prison term when this happened. I hadn't even started my federal penitentiary time yet, but had just done two years in a county lockup waiting for sentencing. So, I sat there in this psycho ward and watched guys assault, kill, and rape each other, or commit suicide, and feel such intense hatred and hostility in that holding cell, but yet I was feeling the happiest I had ever been in my whole life. I was just crying from joy and freedom. I knew something was happening that went beyond anything that I had ever heard of, and I can only call it a Shift to the fourth dimension.

I can remember instances before this in my life when I had done some really good acid, maybe mixed with a little Ecstasy, and created a cocktail that took me out of this feeling of separation for a few hours where I felt some minor sense of freedom. But the true freedom of the Shift is the full nectar that doesn't go away.

The first thing that I noticed in this whole experience of the Shift was that all fear vanished. Now, what I have since found out is that fear doesn't necessarily leave everyone. Other people still have fears, where I may still have frustration, for example. But my memorable experience is of Shifting in prison—my moment-to-moment fear that I might be killed just went away one day and never came back.

Lynn Marie: If you can be free of fear there, you can be free of fear anywhere! Were you seeking freedom at that time? Were you a spiritual seeker before this Shift?

Nadeen: The last thing I could care about in prison was a Shift, or God, or anything else spiritual. I just wanted to stay alive and get out of that prison .

John: But you had in fact been a seeker.

Nadeen: Only all my life. I was intensely interested in the spiritual. I searched through the Catholic priesthood for 14 years. Didn't find what I was looking for, so I jumped from Western to Eastern mysticism. There I lived in ashrams, kissed guru's feet, and did *zazen* 13 hours a day. Doesn't that sound like a typical seeker? Then I went to the other polarity. I went as deep as you can into the third-dimensional world of money, power, drugs, and sex. But the longing to go "home" and know the thoughts of God never left me until the day I woke up. Until that day, everything I did was part of the search.

You see, the passport to this Shift, besides being human, is the intense yearning to go home. All who have Shifted have this yearning in common, and they don't even know where home is. It's like that movie *Close Encounters of the Third Kind,* where the music kept drawing the chosen ones, attracting them, pulling them closer and closer to one center. And then when they get there, they finally know what it is, but not before.

Source is obviously having a very different experience in the last ten years or so, than has ever appeared in recorded history. Right now, instead of only a handful of people remembering who they are, millions of people are attracted to this home of oneness, remembrance of who they really are. Millions, instead of a few!

John: What makes you say "millions"?

Nadeen: There are two reasons: One was my first intuitive hit, which I put in the first book, that it was one percent of the population. Then, after I got out and checked around, I saw that the seekers in the world actually do make up one percent of the population. When I started to do all these intensives and got to share with people everywhere in Satsang, the only people showing up were the intense seekers. These people are not dilettantes or lightweights. These are people living on the edge, where the longing is so intense that it is more important than their career, their relationships, or even their health. Such intense, intense longing that only their tears provided a sure clue of the Shift in progress.

John: Sounds like us. [Laughter]

Nadeen: Yes, that's one of the signs we all share. And the other interesting thing that we all share is the precursor to the Shift—the dark night of the soul. I have found that to be virtually universal. I wish I could say that I've met one person who says, "Ah, I am living here in the fourth dimension and haven't yet had a dark night of the soul." The dark night is a feeling that you go through at some point of being totally flat—in your business, relationships, and hobbies. It's worse than feeling flat; you feel despair. It feels like both God and your common sense have abandoned you, and your value systems are zip. And this is the crumbling of the ego, which identifies with the mind. The experience of disidentification seems to use a dark night of the soul as its process. I haven't met a person who doesn't go through some sort of incredible crushing of everything they thought they were. You won't do this on your own! You won't go off to a Zen monastery and say, "Okay, I want to crush my personality now." The mind doesn't give up that easily; it's not supposed to. All the old conditioning has to be crushed and overcome by something other than the mind. I call this the dark night of the soul. This is the part that people don't want to hear about.

John: I just want to clarify something. You have traveled rather extensively—you mentioned 78 cities in the last 2½ years and seeing about 10,000 people in Satsang—and you are saying that this same awakening process is happening in everyone?

Nadeen: It is happening to seekers who share that longing to know God, and languages don't matter—it is exactly the same all over Europe, Canada, the United States, and South America. We are talking about the Shift, the intensity of the longing, the dark night of the soul, remembering the beginning of who you are, and then the gradual embracing of life as it is. Everyone at Satsang nods, saying, "Yes, this is my experience, too." It's universal.

Lynn Marie: You are validating our vision and intention with our book, which is to show that the phenomenon of awakening is happening at this time and that it is possible to experience this. And there may be people reading this who have that yearning, and they may be wondering what they can do. They may be asking themselves, "Am I going crazy? What do I do about this?" Do you have any suggestions for them?

Nadeen: Just one: Do nothing! [Laughter] Awakening can't occur where there is a doer trying to make it happen. Yet if the mind is involved, there is a doer, by Source's plan. If you are feeling this longing and wonder, "Is this my Shift or my midlife crisis?" then please know this: It is the Shift, because it is happening simultaneously to every seeker on the planet right now. It is amazing to walk into a room of three or four hundred people whom I don't know and who don't know me. But when I start talking about this, they are crying, sobbing, getting up and passing the mike, saying, "This is exactly what I am feeling and going through right now." Usually, it is still mixed in with a lot of concepts about how it is supposed to be, but we get past these in the intensives. It's easy to get rid of them. What you can't get rid of is the longing, until you are finally home.

Another amazing thing that I'm finding out is that there are people who have been intense seekers their whole life—done everything, been to India, followed masters, you name it—until the longing became just unbearable. But then one day, that longing suddenly went away and never came back. This is the only sudden thing in the whole process. The longing just disappears the day you remember who you are. Now, your deliverance has begun. The miracle is that something so strong, which has driven you for 30, 40, or 50 years, can disappear in a night or during a weekend intensive. That's when you don't care anymore if you ever Shift or wake up. You feel like you are coming home and there is nothing else to do. I can't tell you how many times I have seen that. It is such a beautiful thing to see people sob tears and tears of relief because their search is over, and there's nothing left to do. It is not because I told them this. You can't recognize anything someone tells you unless you already know it. But when you validate what they already know at some deep level, the Shift occurs in the sense that the longing stops. This cessation of the longing seems totally illogical in the face of a whole lifetime of seeking.

Lynn Marie: At that point what you call the deliverance begins. Would you say more about what you mean by deliverance?

Nadeen: What is keeping you from the Shift in the first place are concepts—how life "should be." You have been programmed in a number of ways, the strongest being your predispositions. Everyone has unique strands of DNA that make them totally different from any other person in the universe. As I've mentioned before, the biggest thing I got out of the Clinton-Lewinsky scandal was when they tested the famous blue dress to see if the DNA was Clinton's. Sure enough, there was a 7.5 trillion-to-one accuracy rate—*trillion!* That means that in a million planet Earths, each with as many people as we have now, there still wouldn't be a duplicate—there is only one Bill Clinton. And that is how unique each one of us is. These predispositions come with us into this world where they are programmed by society into concepts about how life should be. This is the barrier between the third and fourth dimensions—and the breakthrough is the remembrance that you are this consciousness, this Source. Then begins the gradual breaking down of every concept that you have had from the beginning of time. It won't end until the day you die. However, with each new contraction you have, there is an embrace of the contraction and the Witness saying "yes" to the no. In that process a concept dissolves; every time you have a contraction and you meet it with awareness, something dissolves and never comes back.

Lynn Marie: And by "contraction," you mean a resistance to what is?

Nadeen: It's a strongly felt "no" to what is. Your tape recorder isn't working right, and you say "no" inside. That's a contraction, a little bitty one in the scale of things, but it's a still a "no." And in the middle of this contraction there is a Witness saying, "All is well." That's the miracle of the Shift. The big secret of the Shift is that your deliverance happens not through blissing out and going into nirvana, but with awareness in the middle of a contraction. It happens when, in the middle of the "no" of a contraction, there is the "yes" of the Witness happening at the same time. The reason it is so miraculous is that the Witness sees through the contraction and doesn't buy it. It just says, "Ah, look, anger is present." Only the Witness can say "yes" to "no," or even to "Hell, no." That's not possible without the grace of what I call the Shift, or awareness of the fourth dimension. How many contractions do we get in a day—20, 30, or 40? You'll never run out of contractions. Your deliverance will always go on. And guess what? It always gets better; it only gets better. It's never as good as it gets.

Lynn Marie: It is wonderful for me to hear you articulate this, because it is becoming more and more my own experience. Once awareness was recognized, I was able to relax here and let everything just kind of happen more. The resting is occurring in a wider range of situations—or contractions, as you would say—all the time. I am more able to allow everything to just be as it is, instead of trying to push things away or keep them a certain way. I am beginning to discover that I don't need to try to keep the mind quiet in order to be peaceful. The awareness is the peacefulness, and it's always here, no matter what the mind is doing. What's amazing is that there's no need to get rid of anything I experience or any part of who I am. I have spent so much of my life working so hard on changing who I am. It's a surprise and a relief to be discovering that it's all perfect, just as it is. Just leave it alone; just be. So simple.

Nadeen: All who are in the Shift are sharing this same experience. The curiosity of those in the Shift is all the same. We all have the same questions. We all talk about the same things. Sometimes I don't know what city I'm in, because they're all the same. Nothing is ever different.

John: Two or three years ago, the focus of the questions in Satsang was, "What are you talking about?" and "How can I see what you're talking about?" Now, more and more what we hear is, "How can I stabilize in this recognition? How can I keep it no matter what? I seem to lose it in different situations." Now, more people have had the awakening recognition and want to know how to stay with the experience of awakeness in the stress of everyday modern life. Can you address this?

Nadeen: They're confused. They are expecting a trouble-free existence. What they don't know is that the fourth dimension lies in the middle of the contractions. They're trying to stay in a space where they feel bliss, freedom, joy, and oneness, but it can't be that way all the time. The law of balance prevails, meaning that your life is going to be as much freedom as it is limitation. This doesn't mean that you identify with the limitation side of it, or even the freedom side of it. These people have had what I would call peak experiences. The nature of a peak experience is that it comes, it goes, and then you try to get it back. That's not what we're talking about here. That's not the Shift; it's a peak experience. It's part, a glimpse, of the Shift, but the real heart of the Shift is a deep pervading Presence that never leaves you and is always available in the middle of every contraction—a deep safety net of knowing who you are and that all is well. This never goes. Peak experiences come and go. Limitations and contractions come and go. The Presence never goes. Whenever you want, the Witness is always there. This is the part that you wouldn't trade for anything outside of you in the whole world—this Presence that never, ever leaves you.

The deepest experience in the whole Shift is just being ordinary and neutral. Now neutral sounds like a very boring place. But it's the most incredible, delicious experience available because you're not looking for the highs and not bummed out by the lows. You're in this deep valley that is unaffected by bliss or disappointment. Bliss can distract you as much as disappointment can. People are looking for the bliss, and they're looking down the wrong alley. They are still confused, but they will understand eventually in time.

John: I believe that this confusion happens because when awakening first occurs, very often there is incredible bliss at the release. The revelation is then associated with bliss rather than the recognition of the spacious presence which is just here, no matter what the experience. It's so simple, effortless, and ordinary. But the release into the recognition can be dramatic.

Nadeen: It's a relief from the pressure of not having to perform, achieve, or maintain anything. But that goes quickly. The most bliss I've ever heard about in sharing Satsang stories with 10,000 people is maybe three weeks. After that it comes and goes, but it usually doesn't come and go in three-week increments. I also had about a three-week bliss out; I just cried from relief and joy at knowing I was home. Then life got real again, but it was totally different. Now I wasn't identifying with the judgments. I was shocked when I had my first judgment. I thought, "How could I have experienced this bliss so strongly and still be judging a guard for beating up that inmate?" I wanted to go kill him—I was so mad. My biggest recognition was an acceptance of life as it is. Here is a guard brutally beating up an inmate, and on the one hand I was angry and judgmental, but the real identity saw that this is just as it is, and it's okay. The mind was going crazy trying to figure this out. With deliverance I learned, "Forget the mind. It's not going to figure it out." It's not supposed to figure it out. Not now, not ever!

Lynn Marie: There are many misunderstandings about enlightenment. One is what we were just discussing—that enlightenment is constant bliss. . . .

Nadeen: Up until recently, no one has ever told the whole story about what enlightenment really is. Everything you've ever read in your whole life about enlightenment, that was written before ten years ago, is more of a fairy tale than factual reality. Historically, authors have been telling stories about the glory side of enlightenment that aren't true. When you get down to the nitty-gritty of what it means to live in the fourth dimension, you're talking about things like embracing, accepting, and dancing yes in the middle of no—instead of *siddhis* or supernatural powers, mystical insights, or psychic abilities. These are all phenomena. They come and go and mean nothing to your personal happiness—nothing. The key to your deep, lasting, permanent happiness is accepting life just as it is. And you cannot do that as a human being unless you're Shifted.

Lynn Marie: It sounds extreme to me to say that everything ever written about enlightenment before ten years ago was a complete fairy tale. The old masters knew something. They were experiencing enlightenment as it was at that time. Now it is expanding and evolving, but that doesn't mean that everything they said is not true.

Nadeen: The problem here is that it wasn't the masters who were necessarily writing about their own experience of enlightenment.

It was their devotees or investigative biographers, as it were, putting down on paper what they imagined that the master was experiencing, as interpreted by their own filters of mind and their own third-dimensional experience of life. For whatever reasons of destiny, somehow even the masters managed to slip into their message of enlightenment enough do's and don'ts to lose the "total freedom" side of this message. Until now it hasn't been timely or appropriate for Source to completely reveal how Consciousness can simultaneously dwell with one foot in the third dimension and one in the fourth. Source has finally come clean with this Shift!

John: Saying yes to everything that happens in life brings up the issue of suffering. There is an incredible amount of suffering in the world today, really horrific things occurring every day to many people. How do we say "yes" to this, too?

Nadeen: All suffering in the world, without exception, is the mind judging that life should be otherwise. Even something like physical pain is not suffering; it's a grace. If there are people suffering out there because their mind is doing the job it was designed to do, then they don't need fixing. That's destiny, that's happening just as it is. That's Source operating at a level where the mind can't understand, but it's going crazy just trying to understand it. When you Shift, nothing changes as far as the number of contractions you are going to have every day. The difference is that because you don't identify with them and you don't try to fix them, you don't suffer. When I cannot relate to my own suffering, then I can't relate to other people's suffering. I don't see people suffering. I see all the craziness going on in Yugoslavia right now, and I know Source is whipping it up into something juicy. I don't know why. I'm not supposed to know why. Don't know, don't care; these are the favorite words of my Witness to my mind. Every time someone asks me a question in Satsang about the suffering in the world I say, "Don't know, don't care." It has nothing to do with me. It doesn't mean I don't empathize or feel compassion, but there is nothing I can do to fix it.

Every question you are asking me is so relevant that I applaud your clarity. I have gone into it very deeply in [this] book, exactly the same line of reasoning because these were questions that challenged me.

In [this] book, I discuss the myths of enlightenment. There are five different kinds of people I meet in my intensives. There are those who say, "It could happen to others, but it can't happen to me," or "This could happen someday, but it couldn't happen now." And I meet people who say, "Everything I know about spiritual enlightenment says that you have to do something to get it. You're not saying anything about doing or meditation. So, this is too simple to be true because there's no doing involved." Then there's the people who are tradition-oriented and say that you have to have a master or guru, a teaching, and disciplines. Finally, some people question this Shift because either I or others describing the experience don't look like the image that they had expected of an awakened person. I just go through every objection; they all basically stem from the one central point that it is too simple to be true.

Lynn Marie: There is something I would like to address about the many concepts regarding enlightenment. It seems that when you establish set ideas about how it occurs—such as Shifting to the fourth dimension, dark night of the soul, deliverance, and so on—and you say that this is the only way it happens in all cases, this is itself a creation of new concepts. You may be getting rid of some old concepts, but aren't you creating new ones?

Nadeen: First of all, every single word out of my mouth is a concept, meaning that whatever I can say, the opposite is also just as true. That is the universal law of polarity that defines the third dimension. So I would never, ever say that the norms we talk about are "the only way" the Shift can happen. Source loves diversity and contrast. Anything is possible. What [this] book describes are general norms that happen to most people caught up in the Shift.

John: Is there anything else you would like to add?

Nadeen: In my life, within my own Shift and deliverance, which began almost six years ago, I am more and more grateful every day for whatever it is that keeps cranking up the awe and passion in my life. This is the understanding and knowing every day that there is a process going on within me of embracing life as it happens. This is not something that I can do. It is just happening more and more. Embracing life just as it is and watching this mind, which in the beginning was going crazy with objections, fade into almost nothing. Life is so funny and so simple. The real mystery of life lies in its simplicity, not in its complexity. This is so simple that people can't believe it. You would never have looked here in the middle of contractions for perfect happiness. You would have looked to fixing the suffering of others or fixing your own suffering as the logical place to go. Then when you embrace the events of life just as they are, life has a way of turning right around and providing you with your own happiness from within. This is the most surprise ending you could ever hope for in the comic book and soap opera of life.

John: Thank you very much. It's wonderful to be with you.

chapter 29

The Wisdom of the
Ashtavakra Gita

As the final chapter in my first book, I quoted a few verses of Lao Tzu's *Tao Te Ching*. I did this just in case anyone out there might think that there really is any new wisdom under the sun. But what is new is that because of this force field of new energy available called the Shift, maybe we are now ready to listen to some ancient wisdom, or even better, to finally understand it.

The *Ashtavakra Gita* is another book of short verses that is packed with incredible wisdom. I remember reading it before my Shift and wondering what it was all about. Like the *Tao Te Ching*, it has also been around since before the time of Buddha, Christ, or Mohammed. Instead of coming out of China, this one originated in India, given by an anonymous master of the Advaita Vedanta school of Shankara. What is contained here in poetic little verses is the essence of what you yourself will experience as this Shift sweeps you away from conventional conditioning and concepts.

The feedback from thousands of readers of *Onions* is that Lao Tzu's verses were like a dainty dessert of wonderful tidbits at the end of a meal of strange new spiritual food. It was delightful that so many ran down to their local bookstore and bought the whole book of complete verses, once their appetite was whetted.

That might happen again here. Every single word, without exception, describes so poetically what I have tried to explain about the Shift with many voluminous chapters. Before the Shift I just didn't get it. Now, not only does every word make perfect sense, but it also delights me with its simplicity. The translation of the original Sanskrit was done by Thomas Byron and was published by Shambhala Publications in 1990, titled *The Heart of Awareness*. I hope you feel a tingle of inner excitement when these verses resonate with the Wisdom of your Witness.

The Self

O Master,
Tell me how to find
Detachment, wisdom, and
   freedom!

If you wish to be free,
Know you are the Self,
The witness of all these,
The heart of awareness.

Set your body aside.
Sit in your own awareness.

You will at once be happy,
Forever still,
Forever free.

Formless and free,
Beyond the reach of the sens-
es,
The witness of all things

So be happy!

Right or wrong,
Joy and sorrow,
They are not yours.

It is not really you
Who acts or enjoys.

You are everywhere,
Forever free.

Forever and truly free,
The single witness of all
   things.

But if you see yourself as
   separate.

Then you are bound.

Know you are one,
Pure awareness.

With the fire of this conviction,
Burn down the forest of
   ignorance.

Free your self from sorrow,
And be happy.

Meditate on the self.
One without two,
Exalted awareness.

❧

Awareness

Yesterday
I lived bewildered,
In illusion.

But now I am awake,
Flawless and serene,
Beyond the world.

Now I have given up
The body and the world,
I have a special gift.

I see the infinite Self.
Like the sugar
In the juice of the sugarcane,
I am the sweetness

Two from one!
This is the root of suffering.

Only perceive
That I am one without two,
Pure awareness, pure joy,
And all the world is false.

There is no other remedy!

Through ignorance
I once imagined I was bound.

But I am pure awareness.

I live beyond all distinctions,
In unbroken meditation.
        (Presence)

            ***

The True Seeker

The wise man knows the Self,
And he plays the game of life.

But the fool lives in the world
Like a beast of burden.

He understands the nature of
        things.
His heart is not smudged
By right or wrong,
As the sky is not smudged by
        smoke.

He is pure of heart,
He knows the whole world is
        only the Self.
So who can stop him
From doing as he wishes?

            ❧

The Mind

The mind desires this,
And grieves for that.
It embraces one thing,
And spurns another.

Now it feels anger,
Now happiness.

In this way you are bound.

But when the mind desires
        nothing
And grieves for nothing,

When it is without joy or
    anger
And, grasping nothing,
Turns nothing away . . .

Then you are free.

Where there is no I,
You are free.

Where there is I,
You are bound.

Consider this.

It is easy.

Embrace nothing,
Turn nothing away.

Nothing lasts.
Nothing is real.
Know this.
Give it up.
Be still.

Let go of all contraries.
Whatever comes, be happy

And so fulfill yourself.

Masters, saints, seekers:
They all say different things.

Whoever knows this,
With dispassion becomes quiet.

The true master considers well.
With dispassion
He sees all things are the
    same.

He comes to understand
The nature of things,
The essence of awareness.

Let them all go.
Hold on to nothing.

Every good fortune,
Wives, friends, houses, lands,
All these gifts and riches . . .

They are a dream,
A juggling act,
A traveling show!

A few days, and they are gone.
Let them all go.
Hold on to nothing.

Stillness

All things arise,
Suffer change,
And pass away.
This is their nature.

When you know this,
Nothing perturbs you,
Nothing hurts you.

You become still.
It is easy.

God made all things.
There is only God.

When you know this,
Desire melts away.

Clinging to nothing,
You become still.

Sooner or later,
Fortune or misfortune
May befall you.

When you know this,
You desire nothing,
You grieve for nothing.

Whatever you do
Brings joy or sorrow,
Life or death.

When you know this,
You may act freely,
Without attachment.

For what is there to
    accomplish?

All sorrow comes from fear.
From nothing else.

When you know this,
You become free of it,
And desire melts away.

You become happy
And still.
"I am not the body,
Nor is the body mine.
I am awareness itself."

When you know this,
You have no thought
For what you have done
Or left undone.

You become one,
Perfect and indivisible.

"I am in all things,
From Brahma to a blade of
    grass."

When you know this,
You have no thought

For success or failure
Or the mind's inconstancy.

You are pure.
You are still.

Meditation is needed
Only when the mind is
    distracted
By false imagining.

Knowing this,
I am *fulfilled.*

Doing or not doing,
Both come from not knowing.

Knowing this fully,
I am fulfilled.

I accept nothing.
I reject nothing.

And I am happy.

Knowing I do nothing,
I do whatever comes my way,
And I am happy.

Bound to his body,
The seeker insists on striving
Or on sitting still.

But I no longer suppose
The body is mine,
Or is not mine.

And I am happy.

Sleeping, sitting, walking,
Nothing good or bad befalls
me.

I sleep, I sit, I walk,
And I am happy.

Struggling or at rest,
Nothing is won or lost.

I have forsaken the joy of
    winning
And sorrow of losing.

And I am happy.

For pleasures come and go.
How often I have watched
    their inconstancy!

The Fool

Without, a fool.
Within, free of thought.

I do as I please,
And only those like me
Understand my ways.

~✤~

The Clear Space of Awareness

Detached from the senses,
You are free.

Attached, you are bound

When this is understood,
You may live as you please.

When this is understood,
The man who is bright and
     busy
And full of fine words
Falls silent.

He does nothing.
He is still.

No wonder
Those who wish to enjoy the
     world
Shun this understanding!

You are not your body.
Your body is not you.

You are not the doer.
You are not the enjoyer.

You are pure awareness,
The witness of all things.

You are without expectation,
Free.

Wherever you go,
Be happy.

If the body lasted till the end
     of time,
Or vanished today,
What would you win or lose?

You are the endless sea
In whom all the worlds like
     waves
Naturally rise and fall.

You have nothing to win,
Nothing to lose.

So who are you to think
You can hold on to it,
Or let it go?

How could you!

The world only arises from
    ignorance.
You alone are real.

There is no one,
Not even God,
Separate from your self.

You are pure awareness.

You find peace.

Never upset your mind
With yes and no.

Be quiet.
You are awareness itself.

What is the use of thinking?

Once and for all,
Give up meditation.
Hold nothing in your mind.

You are the Self,
And you are free.

Forget Everything

My Child,
You may read or discuss
    scripture
As much as you like.

But until you forget everything,
You will never live in your
    heart.

Striving is the root of sorrow.

But who understands this?

Only when you are blessed
With the understanding of this
    teaching
Will you find freedom.

Seeing to this,
Neglecting that . . .

But when the mind stops
    setting
One thing against another,
It no longer craves pleasure.

It no longer cares for wealth
Or religious duties or
    salvation.

When desire persists,
Feelings of preference arise,
Of liking and disliking.

They are the root and
    branches of the world.

⁓❦⁓

Beyond All

The man who knows the truth
Is never unhappy in the world.

For he alone fills the universe.

It is hard to find
A man who has an open mind,
Who neither seeks nor shuns
Wealth or pleasure,
Duty or liberation,
Life or death . . .

He does not want the world
    to end.
He does not mind if it lasts.

Whatever befalls him,
He lives in happiness.

For he is truly blessed.

Now that he understands,
He is fulfilled.

He sees and he hears,
He touches and smells and
    tastes,
And he is happy.

And whoever draws near him,
A woman full of passion
Or Death Himself,
He is not shaken.

He stays in his heart.

He is free indeed!

It is all the same to him.
Man or woman,
Good fortune or bad,
Happiness or sorrow.

It makes no difference.
He is serene.

The world no longer holds him.
He has gone beyond
The bounds of human nature.

Without compassion
Or the wish to harm,
Without pride or humility.

Nothing disturbs him.
Nothings surprises him.

Because he is free,
He neither craves nor disdains
The things of the world.

He takes them as they come.

His mind is always detached.

His mind is empty.
He is not concerned with
    meditation,
Or the absence of it,
Or the struggle between good
    and evil.

He is beyond all,
Alone.

His mind has stopped
    working!
It has simply melted away . . .
And with it,
Dreams and delusions and
    dullness.

And for what he has become,
There is no name.

Finding freedom in this life,
The seeker takes nothing to
    heart,

Neither duty nor desire.

He has nothing to do
But to live out his life.

When you are distracted,
You practice concentration.

But the master is undistracted.

He has nothing to fulfill.
What is there left for him to
    accomplish?

He acts like an ordinary man.
But inside he is quite different.

He sees no imperfection in
    himself,
No distraction,
Nor any need for meditation.

He is awake,
Fulfilled,
Free from desire.

He neither is nor is not.

He looks busy,
But he does nothing.

Striving or still,
He is never troubled.

He does whatever comes
    his way,
And he is happy.

He has no desires.
He has cast off his chains.
He walks on air.

He has gone beyond the world,
Beyond joy and sorrow.

His mind is always cool.
He lives as if he had no body.

His mind is cool and pure.
He delights in the Self.

There is nothing he wishes to
    renounce.
He misses nothing.

He mind is naturally empty.
He does as he pleases.

He is not an ordinary man.
Honor and dishonor mean
    nothing to him.

He finds freedom in this life,
But he acts like an ordinary
man.

Yet he is not a fool.

Happy and bright,
He thrives in the world.

Undistracted,
He does not meditate.

Unbound,
He does not seek freedom.

Even when he is still,
The selfish man is busy.

Even when he is busy,
The selfless man is still.

When a fool hears the truth,
He is muddled.

When a wise man hears it,
He goes within.

He may look like a fool,
But he is not muddled.

Striving or still,
The fool never finds peace.

But the master finds it
Just by knowing how things are.

In this world
Men try all kinds of paths.

But they overlook the Self,
The Beloved.

The fool will never find
    freedom
By practicing concentration.

But the master never fails.

Just by knowing how things are,
He is free and constant.

Because the fool wants to
    become God,
He never finds him.

The master is already God,
Without ever wishing to be.

Because the fool looks for
    peace,
He never finds it.

But the master is always at
    peace,
Because he understands how
    things are.

When a man realizes
He is neither the doer nor the
    enjoyer,
The ripples of his mind are
    stilled.

The master goes about his
    business
With perfect equanimity.

He is happy when he sits,
Happy when he talks and eats,
Happy asleep,
Happy coming and going.

Because he knows his own
    nature,
He does what he has to with
    out feeling ruffled
Like ordinary people.

His sorrows are at an end.

～≈९～

About the Author

Satyam Nadeen resides in the Atlanta area. He travels extensively throughout the world facilitating Satsang and monthly hold retreats at one of his centers in either Costa Rica, Tulum, Mexico, or in the Blue Ridge Mountains of North Georgia. For info on these centers: www.rrresorts.com.

You may contact Satyam Nadeen by writing or calling:

New Freedom Press
P.O. Box 1496
Conyers, GA. 30012
Telephone: 888-363-3738
Fax: 770-785-9260

Please visit Nadeen's website at:
www.satyamnadeen.com

Notes

Notes

Notes

Notes

Notes

To learn more about the

BEYOND ENLIGHTENMENT: Abiding in the Zone

Intensives and Retreats with Nadeen,

audio- and videocassettes, and New Freedom

electronic newsletter, check everything

that applies, fill out your address information, attach

postage, and mail card

YES! Please send me information on the following:

❑ U.S. weekend Intensives   ❑ Audiocassettes of Intensives

❑ 7-day retreats in Costa Rica   ❑ Free quaterly electronic
                                              New Freedom newsletter

❑ DVD's of Satsangs

Name _____

Address _____

City _____ State _____ Zip _____

Daytime telephone number _____

E-mail _____

To:

NEW FREEDOM PRESS
P.O. Box 1496
Conyers, GA 30012